PRACTICE TESTS

for

Carlson • Buskist

Psychology
The Science of Behavior

Fifth Edition

prepared by

William Buskist
Auburn University

Allyn and Bacon
Boston · London · Toronto · Sydney · Tokyo · Singapore

Copyright © 1997 by Allyn & Bacon
A Viacom Company
160 Gould Street
Needham Heights, Massachusetts 02194

Internet: www.abacon.com
America Online: keyword: College Online

All rights reserved. No part of the material protected by this copyright notice may be reproduced or utilized in any form or by any means, electronic or mechanical, including photocopying, recording, or by any information storage and retrieval system, without the written permission of the copyright owner.

ISBN 0-205-27140-5

Printed in the United States of America

10 9 8 7 6 5 4 3   01 00 99 98 97

To the Student

This booklet contains two practice tests for each chapter in your textbook, *Psychology: The Science of Behavior, Fifth Edition*, authored by Neil R. Carlson and William Buskist. Each practice test contains 12 multiple-choice questions. Immediately following the practice tests for each chapter are the corresponding answer keys. In addition to the correct letter answer for each question, the answer keys also provide a brief explanation of why that answer is correct. Corresponding textbook pages are referenced for each answer.

You may be wondering about what would be an effective way to incorporate these practice tests into your study of introductory psychology this term. Here is the advice I give to my own students:

- Read the assigned chapter thoroughly and well in advance of the "real" test over its contents. Take notes over important points and terms either in the margin of your book or on a pad of paper.

- Take the first practice quiz for that chapter.

- Grade the practice test, making special note of questions that you missed or had a difficult time answering.

- Return to your book and reread the sections of the text that correspond to those questions you missed or had difficulty answering.

- A day or so later, take the second practice quiz for that chapter.

- Repeat the process for grading it and addressing missed and difficult questions.

- The practice quizzes are not intended to be a substitute for actually reading and studying your text. Rather, their purpose is to allow you to pretest your level of understanding of each chapter so that you can identify aspects of the material that you need to study further.

Following the above procedure for studying the text will aid you in becoming familiar with each chapter's most important points and concepts as well as helping you adapt to the kinds of questions that may appear on your instructor's quizzes or examinations.

Best wishes for a successful and enjoyable academic term.

William Buskist
Auburn, Alabama

Practice Tests
CHAPTER 1: Practice Test 1

1.1. Events that cause other events are known as _____ events.
   a. casual
   b. explanatory
   c. causal
   d. deterministic

1.2. Behaviors such as courting, mating, and parenting are most likely to be studied by a _____ psychologist.
   a. cognitive
   b. personality
   c. comparative
   d. clinical

1.3. That behavior involves mental processes such as attention, perception, and thinking is a view likely to be held by
   a. behavior analysts.
   b. comparative psychologists.
   c. physiological psychologists.
   d. cognitive psychologists.

1.4. The kind of psychologist that you might expect to find in a supermarket or mall studying patterns of shopping behavior is called a(n) _____ psychologist.
   a. consumer
   b. clinical
   c. human factors
   d. organizational

1.5. The subfield of psychology whose primary goals include the study of the workplace is called _____ psychology.
   a. organizational
   b. community
   c. health
   d. consumer

1.6. The best means that we have available to us to study behavior and other natural phenomena objectively is
   a. the philosophy of dualism.
   b. experimental psychology.
   c. the scientific method.
   d. unbiased observation and measurement.

1.7. According to Descartes, _____ are reactions that do not require the use of the mind.
   a. stimulus-response connections
   b. involuntary spinal movements
   c. animistic gestures and movements
   d. reflexes

1.8. The philosopher who rejected the notion that ideas were an innate part of the human mind was
    a. Descartes.
    b. Locke.
    c. Berkeley.
    d. Mill.

1.9. The method of experimental ablation was pioneered by
    a. Hitzig.
    b. Flourens.
    c. Fritsch.
    d. Helmholtz.

1.10. The approach adopted by Wundt for investigating psychological phenomena was
    a. structuralism.
    b. functionalism.
    c. Gestalt psychology.
    d. behaviorism.

1.11. One important contribution to the experimental study of memory credited to Ebbinghaus was his
    a. use of a control group.
    b. use of statistics to determine the significance of his findings.
    c. development of the first stringent test of word recognition.
    d. method for reducing variable error.

1.12. Which two of the following approaches to psychology were most likely to reject the idea that mental events are an appropriate subject matter for study in psychology?
    a. functionalism and behaviorism.
    b. structuralism and behaviorism.
    c. Gestalt psychology and functionalism
    d. structuralism and functionalism.

Practice Tests
CHAPTER 1: Practice Test 2

1.13. Understanding how a drug affects the brain and nervous system is a quest mostly likely to be undertaken by a(n) _____.
   a. developmental psychologist
   b. experimental neuropsychologist
   c. comparative psychologist
   d. physiological psychologist

1.14. _____ is the subfield of psychology that investigates the effects of environmental variables on behavior.
   a. Environmental psychology
   b. Behavior analysis
   c. Cognitive psychology
   d. Social psychology

1.15. The branch of psychology that is likely to involve, among other things, the study of cognitive, physiological, and social changes that occur as people grow older is _____ psychology.
   a. social
   b. developmental
   c. personality
   d. clinical

1.16. _____ psychologists are people whose primary interests involve encouraging people to adopt and maintain patterns of behavior that promote fitness and well-being.
   a. Health
   b. School and educational
   c. Sports
   d. Clinical

1.17. Dr. McGlynn is a psychologist who works for a large automobile maker designing safer dashboards. Dr. McGlynn is mostly like a(n) _____ psychologist.
   a. health
   b. organizational
   c. engineering
   d. consumer

1.18. Descartes was a 17th century
   a. court jester.
   b. inventor.
   c. mathematician.
   d. engineer.

1.19. In Descartes's view the distinction between people and other aspects of the natural world was that humans possess a
   a. soul.
   b. cerebral cortex.
   c. knowledge of God.
   d. mind.

1.20. James Mill is known for his support of
a. empiricism.
b. dualism.
c. materialism.
d. rationalism.

1.21. The physiologists who introduced the use of electrical stimulation to map the functions of different parts of the brain were
a. Fritsch and Hitzig.
b. Flourens and Broca.
c. Helmholtz and Weber.
d. Comte and Locke.

1.22. The popularity of structuralism waned in part because
a. the focus in psychology shifted to the study of human behavior.
b. structuralism was proven by physiologists to be a false doctrine.
c. Wundt's theories about human behavior were proven false by the functionalists.
d. the method of introspection was replaced by experimental ablation.

1.23. The emphasis of the functionalist approach was placed squarely on
a. understanding private mental events.
b. discovering the physiological basis of consciousness.
c. the biological significance of behavior.
d. solving the mysteries of the mind.

1.24. Gestalt psychology lost its power as a primary force in psychology because its
a. basic tenets were proved invalid.
b. theory was not testable.
c. major ideas were absorbed into other approaches.
d. goals were subsumed by humanistic psychology.

Practice Test Answers
CHAPTER 1: Practice Test 1

1.1.	c, p. 3	By definition any event that causes the occurrence of another event is called a causal event.
1.2.	c, p. 4	Comparative psychology is the branch of psychology that studies the adaptive significance of behavior, including those involved in courting, mating, and rearing offspring.
1.3.	d, p. 5	Cognitive psychology is the study of mental processes, which include the roles that attention, perception, and thinking play in behavior.
1.4.	a, p. 7	Consumer psychologists are interested in identifying and understanding those variables that affect patterns of consumer behavior, including the purchasing of goods and services.
1.5.	a, p. 7	Organizational psychologists study the variables that influence the behavior of employers and employees in the attempt to improve conditions under which people work.
1.6.	c, p. 8	The rules of scientific inquiry, as embodied in the scientific method, specify that the investigation of any and all phenomena should be as unbiased as possible. The scientific method emphasizes the use of objective methods in the collection, analysis, and interpretation of data.
1.7.	d, p. 9	Descartes believed that energy from the external world reflected back to it through the body's nervous system and muscles.
1.8.	b, p. 10	Locke argued that all knowledge is derived exclusively from experience.
1.9.	b, p. 11	Flourens was a French physiologist who explored the role of the nervous system in controlling movements of different body parts. By surgically removing different parts of the nervous system and noting the corresponding effects on behavior, Flourens was able to provide empirical evidence for the doctrine of specific nerve energies.
1.10.	a, p. 13	Because Wundt's approach to psychology involved the study of the structure of the mind, it was only natural for his approach to be labeled as structuralism.
1.11.	d, p. 14	Ebbinghaus reduced the role of variable errors (errors caused by random fluctuation of experimental conditions) in his research by making repeated observations of the same phenomenon on different occasions.
1.12.	a, p. 15	Behaviorism arose partially from functionalism, which proposed that the operation of the mind, and not mental structures, was the proper subject matter of psychology. Behaviorism went further in its rejection of mental events and urged that psychologists study only observable events.

Practice Test Answers
CHAPTER 1: Practice Test 2

1.13.   d, p. 4   Physiological psychologists study the role that the brain and nervous system play in controlling behavior, and how environmental variables such as the use of drugs affect the operation of the brain and nervous system (and therefore how drugs affect behavior as mediated by the brain and nervous system).

1.14.   b, p. 4   Behavior analysis is the study of how behavior is affected by its consequences.

1.15.   b, p. 5   Any change that people experience as a part of growing older falls under the domain of developmental psychology.

1.16.   a, p. 6   Health psychology both studies and promotes healthy behaviors.

1.17.   c, p. 7   Engineering psychologists study the interaction of people and machines in the attempt to develop safer and more efficient machines.

1.18.   c, p. 8   Descartes lived during the first half of the 17th century and studied and practiced both philosophy and mathematics.

1.19.   d, p. 9   Descartes argued that humans are the only organisms to possess a mind.

1.20.   c, p. 10   Unlike Descartes, Mill argued that the mind was made of material matter and that only by understanding the physical world, which include the mind, could one truly understand the nature of reality.

1.21.   a, p. 11   Fritsch and Hitzig worked together in exploring the use of electrical stimulation to discover the different functions associated with different brain regions.

1.22.   a, p. 13   Structuralists, such as Wundt, were interested in investigating how the elements of consciousness combined to form the mind. However, this approach soon waned because of the emphasis of both functionalism and behaviorism on observable behavior and its adaptive significance.

1.23.   c, p. 14   The functionalist approach to psychology was heavily influenced by the work of Charles Darwin, the first successful proponent of biological evolution. Functionalists were particularly interested in how the mind functions to aid the organism in adapting to changes in its environment.

1.24.   c, p. 17   Unlike structuralism, Gestalt psychology was not plagued by faulty research methods or by problems. Gestalt psychology was supplanted by other perspectives on psychology because its basic ideas, particularly the notion that the whole is more than the sum of its parts, were gradually siphoned off into these other perspectives.

Practice Tests
CHAPTER 2: Practice Test 1

2.1. The first step of the scientific method specifies that a researcher
   a. design the study.
   b. collect the data for the study.
   c. read the relevant literature on related experiments.
   d. formulate a hypothetical causal relation among the variables.

2.2. A set of statements used to explain a set of phenomena is called a(n)
   a. theory.
   b. hypothesis.
   c. experimental agenda.
   d. research program.

2.3. The variable that is measured in an experiment is called the _____ variable.
   a. relational
   b. independent
   c. causal
   d. dependent

2.4. The term used to describe the fallacy committed when we mistakenly believe that we have explained an event by naming it is the _____ fallacy.
   a. naming
   b. nominal
   c. explanatory
   d. descriptive

2.5. A variable that is inadvertently allowed to affect the value of the dependent variable is called a(n) _____ variable.
   a. unreliable
   b. invalid
   c. confounding
   d. nuisance

2.6. A major problem with the "flawed predator" experiment described in the text involved
   a. failure to assign subjects to groups in a random order.
   b. failure to provide an operational definition for the dependent variable.
   c. the original hypothesis as framed by the experimenter.
   d. the order in which stimuli were presented to subjects.

2.7. In essence, random assignment means that
   a. each subject in the study has an equal chance of being assigned to either the control group or the experimental group.
   b. subjects with particular characteristics are eliminated from the study.
   c. subjects with particular characteristics are assigned to particular groups.
   d. neither the subject nor the experimenter is aware of to which groups the subjects have been assigned, and thus do not know which group will be exposed to the independent variable.

2.8. The statistical procedure used to determine the degree of relationship between two variables is called
   a. a t-test.
   b. the range.
   c. correlation.
   d. analysis of variance.

2.9. In psychological research, the term *generality* refers to
   a. adding the results from one study to those from other studies.
   b. obtaining a broad understanding of how different variables are related to each other.
   c. how significant the results of the statistical analysis are.
   d. applying the results obtained from the sample to understanding the behavior of a larger population of individuals.

2.10. Although animal rights activists target animal research, it is clear that
   a. animal researchers have largely ignored them.
   b. they do so merely for publicity.
   c. they do so merely for the money involved.
   d. pets are more often abused than are animals used in research.

2.11. What is the median of the following set of numbers? (13, 19, 27, 12, 29, 18, 55)
   a. 12
   b. 19
   c. 24.7
   d. 29

2.12. Which of the following correlation coefficients represents the strongest correlation?
   a. +.58
   b. +.62
   c. -.66
   d. -.71

Practice Tests
CHAPTER 2: Practice Test 2

2.13. The determination of whether the results of a study are statistically significant occurs during which step of the scientific method?
 a. the communication of the results
 b. the evaluation of the hypothesis through examination of the data collected
 c. the design of the study
 d. the conducting of the study

2.14. The starting point for any science is
 a. a good hypothesis.
 b. a well-conducted experiment.
 c. a good theory.
 d. observation.

2.15. In an experiment, researchers manipulate the _____ of the _____ variable.
 a. value; dependent
 b. truth or falsity; dependent
 c. value; independent
 d. truth or falsity; independent

2.16. In the hypothetical study on self-esteem and susceptibility to propaganda, discussed in the text, members of the experimental group
 a. received no treatment.
 b. experienced loss of self-esteem.
 c. were not tested for susceptibility to propaganda.
 d. were asked to see a counselor because of their loss of self-esteem.

2.17. A confounding variable
 a. is manipulated by the experimenter.
 b. is not manipulated by the experimenter.
 c. is beyond the experimenter's ability to control.
 d. only rarely affects subjects' performance in an experiment.

2.18. In any experiment, the researcher must make sure that only the _____ variable is manipulated.
 a. confounding
 b. independent
 c. dependent
 d. operationally defined

2.19. A study in which the experimenter but not the subject knows the value of the independent variable is called a _____ study.
 a. counterbalanced
 b. single-blind
 c. deceptive
 d. double-blind

2.20. Single-subject research studies
 a. are chiefly used in experimental research.
 b. do not use any method for controlling confounding variables.
 c. are chiefly used in correlational research.
 d. may be used in either experimental or correlational research.

2.21. Which of the following constitutes a contract between the subject and the researcher regarding the subject's participation in the study?
   a. the confidentiality agreement
   b. the informed consent agreement
   c. the full disclosure agreement
   d. the debriefing agreement

2.22. One important reason cited by the text for why cross-cultural research is important is that it
   a. can test the generality of research results across cultures.
   b. can teach us to appreciate the problems faced by other cultures.
   c. can draw us closer together as members of the human family.
   d. provides insight into how to solve our own social and cultural problems.

2.23. The difference between the highest and lowest numbers in a set of numbers is called the
   a. range.
   b. variance.
   c. standard deviation.
   d. difference score.

2.24. The primary reason researchers calculate an inferential statistic on the data that they collect is that they
   a. wish to determine the statistical significance of their results.
   b. wish to prove beyond a doubt that their hypothesis is correct.
   c. desire to establish the reliability and validity of their methodology.
   d. need to in order to get their research published in a professional journal.

Practice Test Answers
CHAPTER 2: Practice Test 1

2.1. d, p. 23   Before a topic can be investigated scientifically, an investigator must first identify the problem that needs to be addressed and propose a hypothesis that can be tested empirically.

2.2. a, p. 24   By definition, a theory is a set of testable statements regarding the relationship between two or more variables.

2.3. d, p. 26   By definition, the variable that is measured in an experiment is called the dependent variable (its value *depends* on the way it is affected by the independent variable).

2.4. b, p. 26   To label or name a phenomenon merely describes that phenomenon; it does not explain it. The mistaken belief that naming a phenomenon also explains it is called the nominal fallacy.

2.5. c, p. 28   To confound means to confuse. In an experiment, a confounding variable is any variable that prevents the research from drawing a valid conclusion about how the independent variable affects the dependent variable. That is, a confounding variable may confuse the true relationship between the independent and dependent variables.

2.6. d, p. 29   The order in which stimuli are presented to subjects in an experiment may cause different subjects to respond in different ways. In the "flawed predator" study described in the text, all stimuli were presented to all subjects in exactly the same order. As a result, some of the subjects' behavior may have habituated to the stimuli (showing less and less of a response as more stimuli were presented).

2.7. a, p. 31   Before researchers expose subjects in the experimental group to the independent variable, they attempt to equate subjects in both the experimental and control groups in terms of personal variables such as intelligence, personality, and other relevant variables. The primary tool researchers use in this effort is random assignment.

2.8. c, p. 34   By definition, correlation is the statistical procedure used to determine the extent to which two variables are related. However, correlation does not imply causation. To determine the extent to which changes in one variable cause changes in another variable, one must manipulate the independent variable and measure its effects on the dependent variable, not merely measure the values of two dependent variables.

2.9. d, p. 37   In psychological research, studies are conducted with samples of subjects. The results are then generalized to the population of individuals from which the sample was drawn. To the extent that the sample is representative of the population, the generalization is valid.

2.10. d, p. 40   The standards that researchers adhere to for the care and treatment of their animal subjects generally exceed those standards exercised by pet owners for the care and treatment of their pets.

2.11. b, p. 42   The median of this data set may be obtained by first listing the numbers in sequential order from smallest to largest and then determining the middle number.

2.12. d, p. 44   The strength of a correlation is determine by its absolute size and not by its valence (the + or - sign).

Practice Test Answers
CHAPTER 2: Practice Test 2

2.13. b, p. 24   Once the data have been collected, they are subjected to statistical analysis, which will inform the researcher about the validity of the hypothesis.

2.14. d, p. 25   Before any phenomenon can be studied, it must first be observed. Observation permits the researcher to formulate hypotheses about variables that may influence the phenomenon.

2.15. c, p. 26   The cornerstone of experimental research is to manipulate the value of the independent variable to determine its effects on the value of the dependent variable.

2.16. b, p. 27   The experimental manipulation in the self-esteem/propaganda study described in the text involved having subjects "accidentally" knock over a stack of color slides. Doing so presumably lowered their self-esteem.

2.17. b, p. 28   A confounding variable is a variable in an experiment that inadvertently affects the dependent variable. Researchers desire to control these variables; the variables that are manipulated in an experiment are called independent variables.

2.18. b, p. 30   In an experiment, the researcher manipulates the independent variable, measures the dependent variable, and controls potential confounding variables.

2.19. b, p. 33   By definition, a single-blind study involves the experimenter, but not the subjects, knowing the value of the independent variable.

2.20. d, p. 36   Any study that involves only one or a few subjects is called single-subject research. This research may be either experimental or correlational in nature.

2.21. b, p. 39   Informed consent is a written statement describing subjects' rights and responsibilities with respect to a particular study and is signed by both subjects and the experimenter.

2.22. a, p. 41   One very useful characteristic of cross-cultural research is that it permits researchers to examine the extent to which the circumstances surrounding particular behaviors in one culture also influence those or similar behaviors in another culture.

2.23. a, p. 43   By definition, the range is the difference between the lowest and highest scores in a set of scores.

2.24. a, p. 45   The sole purpose of calculating inferential statistics is to determine the extent to which a particular finding is the independent variable manipulated by the experimenter.

Practice Tests
CHAPTER 3: Practice Test 1

3.1. Evolutionary events and conditions that affect behavior are called _____ causes.
    a. evolutionary
    b. proximate
    c. ultimate
    d. genetic

3.2. Darwin was the first person to
    a. propose a theory of biological evolution.
    b. propose the idea of natural selection.
    c. amass considerable evidence in favor of biological evolution.
    d. develop the argument that human beings descended from ape-like beings that roamed the earth many thousands of years ago.

3.3. Which of the following is LEAST likely to contribute to reproductive success in the vast majority of modern human beings?
    a. intelligence
    b. charm
    c. wealth
    d. running speed

3.4. The ultimate test of whether natural selection will favor a particular phenotype (and its underlying genotype) is
    a. the nature of the adaptive advantage it confers on organisms.
    b. whether the animal is a mammal or non-mammal.
    c. how often the underlying genes express themselves.
    d. whether the organism's behavior involves feeding or reproduction.

3.5. *Homo habilis* is to _____ as *Homo erectus* is to _____.
    a. fire; cultural traditions
    b. stone tools; fire
    c. cultural traditions; language
    d. bipedalism; cultural traditions

3.6. Homozygous is to _____ as heterozygous is to _____.
    a. different; same
    b. similar; different
    c. fraternal; identical
    d. same; different

3.7. The Cri-du-chat syndrome is
    a. an example of a genetic disorder caused by a mutation.
    b. due to missing genetic material in chromosome pair #5.
    c. a genetic disorder that is unresponsive to any sort of treatment intervention.
    d. all of the above

3.8. A 40-year-old woman comes to you seeking advice about how she might learn whether her unborn child has genetic defect. Your advice, which is correct, is to tell her to ask her doctor about
   a. amniocentesis.
   b. carrier detection.
   c. DNA probes.
   d. recessive lethal genes.

3.9. When "bright" and "dull" strains of rats were reared in enriched environments designed to stimulate learning, _____ in terms of navigating a maze.
   a. the bright rats still outperformed the dull rats
   b. the dull rats now outperformed the bright rats
   c. both groups of rats performed equally as well
   d. both groups still did not perform as well as rats raised in a standard laboratory cage

3.10. The individual who tends to be the more selective or discriminating when choosing a mate is generally the
   a. male.
   b. individual who will make the greater parental investment.
   c. individual who will make the smaller parental investment.
   d. individual who will have the most opportunities for mating.

3.11. High male and low female parental investment is characteristic of
   a. monogamy.
   b. polygyny.
   c. polyandry.
   d. polygynandry.

3.12. Altruistic behavior toward non-relatives is called
   a. inclusive fitness.
   b. reciprocal altruism.
   c. non-kin selection.
   d. personal fitness.

Practice Tests
CHAPTER 3: Practice Test 2

3.13. During Darwin's five year trip on the HMS *Beagle*, he
  a. discovered natural selection.
  b. believed in creationism.
  c. began to develop his theory of biological evolution.
  d. began his research on artificial selection.

3.14. The tendency for some animals to produce more offspring than other animals of the same species is called
  a. evolution.
  b. adaptive significance.
  c. reproductive success.
  d. natural selection.

3.15. Together, variation (at both the genotypic and phenotypic levels) and competition
  a. produce evolutionary change.
  b. minimize the role that natural selection has played in human evolution.
  c. play only a minor role in natural selection, regardless of species.
  d. act directly on an organism's genotype.

3.16. From study of the fossil record and recent developments in genetic research, we now know that
  a. although natural selection applies to other animals, it does not appear to apply to humans.
  b. humans descended from chimpanzees.
  c. humans are genetically related to other mammals.
  d. the evolution of the human species began about 1.5 million years ago.

3.17. Genes contain
  a. DNA.
  b. chromosomes.
  c. proteins.
  d. all of the above

3.18. Although Emily carries the gene for hemophilia, she does not suffer form the disorder. This is because
  a. the active allele for hemophilia is dominant and she has the recessive allele.
  b. the disorder is due to a sex-influenced gene, not a sex-linked gene.
  c. while she carries an allele for the disorder on the X chromosome, she also carries an allele for normal blood clotting on the Y chromosome.
  d. while she carries an allele for the disorder on one X chromosome, she also carries an allele for normal blood clotting on the other X chromosome.

3.19. If a child inherits a healthy recessive allele from one parent and a lethal dominant allele from the other parent, he or she may
  a. lead a normal healthy life.
  b. die during childhood.
  c. die during adulthood.
  d. lead a normal healthy life or die at any time during the life span.

3.20. Heritability is a term used to refer to
   a. inheritability.
   b. the probability that a trait is due to genetic factors.
   c. heredity.
   d. the amount of variability in a trait in a given population that is due to genetic factors.

3.21. If the concordance rates for a particular trait in both MZ and DZ twins are similar, then that trait is likely due to a(n)
   a. genetic variable.
   b. environmental variable.
   c. weak gene-environment interaction.
   d. strong gene-environment interaction.

3.22. Which of the following statements is TRUE?
   a. In polygynous species, males invest more in offspring than females do.
   b. In humans, the costs associated with reproduction is greater for females than for males.
   c. Compared to females, males generally have fewer opportunities to reproduce.
   d. A female's reproductive success is limited ONLY by the number of times she has intercourse.

3.23. Among many non-human animals the key factor involved in the avoidance of incestuous matings is
   a. the ability to recognize close genetic relatives by sight.
   b. migration away from the birthplace.
   c. sexual incompatibility.
   d. the ability to recognize close genetic relatives by smell.

3.24. According to E. O. Wilson,
   a. the purpose of sociobiology is to develop general laws of evolution and the biology of social behavior.
   b. humans share with other mammals a sexual division of labor.
   c. general principles of sociobiology can be expected to apply to humans as well as to animals.
   d. all of the above

Practice Test Answers
CHAPTER 3: Practice Test 1

3.1.   c, p. 53   By definition, ultimate causes are considered to be evolutionary events and conditions that affect behavior.

3.2.   c, p. 55   Although Darwin was not the first individual to propose biological evolution, he was the first to collect extensive physical evidence to support its existence.

3.3.   d, p. 56   Among humans, factors such as intelligence, charm, and especially wealth play an important role in mate selection. Running speed is a physical attribute that is unrelated to mating for the majority of human beings.

3.4.   a, p. 57   When environmental conditions change, only those animals that possess phenotypes (and their corresponding genotypes) adaptive to such changes, will survive and reproduce.

3.5.   b, p. 58   *Homo habilis* made simple tools and *Homo erectus* discovered and used fire.

3.6.   d, p. 63   *Homozygous* means "same" and *heterozygous* means "different."

3.7.   b, p. 65   The cause of the genetic disorder known as Cri-du-chat syndrome is the deletion of genetic material from chromosome #5.

3.8.   a, p. 67   Amniocentesis involves the removal of fetal cells found in the amniotic fluid surrounding the fetus. Once removed, the chromosomes in these cells are studied for abnormalities.

3.9.   c, p. 68   The study by Cooper and Zubek showed that exposure to an enriched environment caused "dull" rats to negotiate a maze as well as "bright" rats. Thus, environmental factors reduced the effects of genetic differences in "brightness" between the two strains of rats.

3.10.   b, p. 72   Because the individual who makes the greater parental investment has more at stake, he or she is generally more discriminating in the choice of a mate than the individual who makes the lesser parental contribution. In many species, including humans, the female makes the greater parental investment and is therefore considered to be more discriminating in choosing a mate.

3.11.   c, p. 75   Polyandry is the mating of one female with more than one male. Among humans, this reproductive strategy is rare. Among many egg-laying species, the male tends the eggs once they are laid by the female.

3.12.   b, p. 77   By definition, altruistic behavior toward non-relatives is called reciprocal altruism.

Practice Test Answers
CHAPTER 3: Practice Test 2

3.13. b, p. 54 — Darwin still believed in creationism while aboard the HMS *Beagle*. It was not until he was back in England and pondering his collection of specimens that he hatched his version of biological evolution.

3.14. d, p. 55 — By definition, natural selection is the tendency of some organisms within a specific population to produce more offspring than other organisms in that population.

3.15. a, p. 58 — Variation among species members in terms of genotypes and their corresponding phenotypes, together with competition for food, territory, and mates, produces differential survival rates among those organisms in terms of natural selection. And natural selection is what causes evolutionary change.

3.16. c, p. 58 — Modern scientific methods in the area of carbon dating and in molecular genetics has permitted researchers to assess the degree of genetic relatedness among humans and other animals. Our closest living relatives appear to be the gorilla and the chimpanzee.

3.17. a, p. 61 — Genes are composed of segments of DNA. Chromosomes contain genes, which code for the synthesis of proteins.

3.18. d, p. 65 — Because females carry two X chromosomes and the gene for hemophilia is located on the X chromosome, females can still have normal blood clotting if only one of the genes for hemophilia is normal. Males who carry only one X chromosome will have hemophilia if it contains the defective gene for blood clotting.

3.19. d, p. 66 — Dominant lethal genes, although rare, can express themselves at any time during the life-span.

3.20. d, p. 68 — By definition, heritability refers to the amount of genetic variability for a specific trait in a given population at a given time.

3.21. b, p. 70 — Because MZ twins share all their genes with each other and DZ twins share only fifty percent of their genes with each other, differences in concordance rates between these types of twins is often considered as evidence that genetic factors play a role in whatever trait is being studied. Likewise, similarities in concordance rates for these types of twins is considered as evidence that environmental factors play a role in whatever trait is being studied.

3.22. b, p. 73 — Because women can have only a limited number of children and bear all of the physical costs associated with pregnancy and the early care of a child, and because men, at a minimum, invest only the time required for impregnation, women are considered to invest more in reproduction than men.

3.23. b, p. 76 — Because members of many animal species leave the territories in which they were born before they become reproductively mature, they seldom, if ever, end up mating with a close genetic relative.

3.24. d, p. 78 — The quote given on page 78 makes Wilson's stand on these issues very clear.

Practice Tests
CHAPTER 4: Practice Test 1

4.1.   The two primary functions of the brain are to
   a. control behavior and regulate the body's physiological processes.
   b. control behavior and monitor thought processes.
   c. control the body's physiological processes and regulate homeostasis.
   d. maintain homeostasis and regulate the processing of information from the environment.

4.2.   One function of the soma is to
   a. secrete transmitter substances.
   b. receive messages from neurons.
   c. carry messages to the dendrites.
   d. to transmit messages to the cell body.

4.3.   The action potential begins in the _____ and is transmitted to the _____.
   a. terminal buttons; end of the axon attached to the soma
   b. end of the axon attached to the soma; terminal buttons
   c. dendrites; terminal buttons
   d. soma; axon

4.4.   One of the most important factors in relating brain lesions to changes in behavior is
   a. how the lesion was produced.
   b. how recently the damaged occurred.
   c. where the lesion is located.
   d. all of the above

4.5.   Brain development
   a. essentially takes place in a vacuum.
   b. is strongly influenced by sex hormones.
   c. is more strongly influenced by heredity factors than environmental factors.
   d. is more strongly influenced by environmental factors than heredity factors.

4.6.   The lobe of the brain located immediately behind the central fissure is called the _____ lobe.
   a. temporal
   b. occipital
   c. medial
   d. parietal

4.7.   Which of the following is NOT likely to result from damage to the prefrontal cortex?
   a. loss of spontaneity
   b. perseveration
   c. inability to plan
   d. loss of intelligence

4.8.   All sensory information EXCEPT _____ is sent to the thalamus before it reaches the cerebral cortex.
   a. olfaction
   b. gustation
   c. vision
   d. audition

4.9. _____ depress brain activity by stimulating a specific neuromodulator receptor.
   a. Amphetamines
   b. Hallucinogenic drugs
   c. Barbiturates
   d. Psychedelics

4.10. Antipsychotic drugs that are effective against schizophrenia
   a. stimulate the reuptake of dopamine.
   b. inhibit the reuptake of dopamine.
   c. duplicate the effects of dopamine.
   d. block dopamine receptors.

4.11. A primary transmitter substance that appears to be affected by the consumption of many hallucinogenic drugs is
   a. serotonin.
   b. dopamine.
   c. acetylcholine.
   d. GABA.

4.12. Marty is a drug addict who is currently experiencing nausea, cramping, and diarrhea. Most likely, Marty is suffering some of the withdrawal symptoms associated with _____ addiction.
   a. cocaine
   b. benzodiazepine
   c. clozapine
   d. heroin

Practice Tests
CHAPTER 4: Practice Test 2

4.13. The part of the brain to evolve most recently is the
   a. brain stem.
   b. limbic system.
   c. cerebellum.
   d. cerebral hemisphere.

4.14. Multiple sclerosis involves the deterioration of the _____ of the neuron.
   a. terminal buttons
   b. myelin sheath
   c. soma
   d. dendrites

4.15. The strength of a muscular contraction is governed by the
   a. number of neurons that control it.
   b. rate of firing of the neurons that control it.
   c. size of the neurons that control it.
   d. type of transmitter substance that is released by the neurons that control it.

4.16. The protein molecule that is located in the membrane of a postsynaptic neuron that allows the neuron to be excited or inhibited by presynaptic neurons is called a
   a. neuromodulator.
   b. transmitter substance.
   c. ion transporter.
   d. receptor molecule.

4.17. That a rat will press a lever to obtain electrical stimulation to a particular region of the brain suggests that
   a. the animal is responding to avoid a punishing stimulus.
   b. the particular area is involved in reward.
   c. the nervous system is electrical in nature.
   d. rats enjoy electrical shock.

4.18. Alison is a very talented gymnast. According to most modern psychologists, her skill in this area most likely represents
   a. a genetic predisposition.
   b. environmental influences.
   c. her desire to excel in the sport.
   d. the interaction of genetic and environmental factors.

4.19. Andy has sustained damage to his right primary motor cortex. He is apt to experience difficulty in movements associated with his
   a. right hand.
   b. left hand.
   c. index finger.
   d. eyes.

4.20. The inability of a person who is not blind to recognize the identity or use of an object by means of vision is termed visual
   a. amnesia.
   b. aphasia.
   c. apraxia.
   d. agnosia.

4.21. Which of the following is NOT a function of the brain stem?
   a. to control species typical behaviors
   b. to regulate homeostasis
   c. to maintain a proper balance of nutrients stored within the body
   d. to regulate postural adjustments

4.22. The transmitter substance, _____, is involved with respiration.
   a. GABA
   b. serotonin
   c. dopamine
   d. acetylcholine

4.23. One of the negative side-effects of abusing cocaine and amphetamine (if taken in large doses over a few days) is
   a. hallucinations.
   b. rapid weight gain.
   c. sexual arousal.
   d. depression.

4.24. If drug addiction were caused purely by physiological addiction to a drug, then people would not become addicted to _____ because consuming this drug does not result in physiological dependence.
   a. cocaine
   b. heroin
   c. morphine
   d. opium

Practice Test Answers
CHAPTER 4: Practice Test 1

4.1.   a, p. 85   Homeostasis, monitoring of thought processes, and the regulation of information processing are subsumed under the control of behavior and the regulation of the body's physiological processes.

4.2.   b, p. 88   The soma, or cell body, receives incoming messages from other neurons. It neither secretes transmitter substances nor carries messages to the dendrites.

4.3.   b, p. 89   Once the soma is stimulated sufficiently, an action potential is generated at the end of the axon attached to it. From there, the action potential travels the entire length of the axon to the terminal buttons, which, in turn, release a transmitter substance into the synaptic cleft.

4.4.   c, p. 98   In order to correlate brain damage to changes in behavior, researchers must know which part of the brain has been damaged.

4.5.   b, p. 101   During prenatal, or fetal, development, sex hormones are secreted that influence particular areas of the brain. Brain development does not occur in a vacuum; both hereditary and environmental stimulation have been shown to affect certain brain regions during early development.

4.6.   d, p. 104   As the illustration on page 104 shows, the parietal lobe is located immediately behind the central fissure. The other lobes are located either in front of, farther behind, or below the central fissure. The description of the parietal lobe given on page 103 also indicates its location.

4.7.   d, p. 107   A person whose prefrontal cortex has been damaged still does fairly well on standard tests of intelligence. However, this person shows decreased spontaneity, an inability to alter problem-solving strategies, and poor planning skills.

4.8.   a, p. 111   The thalamus serves as a relay station for sensory information regarding taste, seeing, and hearing. Sensory information regarding smell travels a different route on its way to the cerebral cortex.

4.9.   c, p. 116   Barbiturates induce sedation by stimulating neuromodulator receptors. Amphetamines are stimulants that prevent reuptake of dopamine and many hallucinogens suppress the activity of serotonin-secreting neurons. Hallucinogens are sometimes referred to as psychedelics.

4.10.   d, p. 116   Some of the symptoms of schizophrenia appear to stem from an overabundance of dopamine. Drugs that block dopamine receptors have been shown to reduce the severity of these symptoms.

4.11.   a, p. 118   Hallucinogenic drugs such as LSD, psilocybin, and DMT suppress the activity of serotonin-secreting neurons, permitting the mechanisms involved in dreaming to become activated. As a result, hallucinations occur during periods of wakefulness.

4.12.   d, p. 119   Marty is suffering from the withdrawal symptoms of heroin because, among the four drugs mentioned, only withdrawal from heroin produces these symptoms.

Practice Test Answers
CHAPTER 4: Practice Test 2

4.13.	d, p. 85	The evolution of the brain has occurred in layers. The brain stem and limbic system are the first two layers, and are thus the oldest parts of the brain. The third layer, the cerebral hemispheres, appear to have evolved more recently.
4.14.	b, p. 89	The immune systems of people who have multiple sclerosis attack a protein that is found in the myelin sheath.
4.15.	b, p. 91	Muscles are made up of thousands of individual fibers. Large groups of motor neurons synapse with particular groups of muscle fibers. When these motor neurons fire at a high rate, the muscle contracts strongly; when they fire at a low rate, the muscle contracts weakly.
4.16.	d, p. 91	A transmitter substance either excites or inhibits a postsynaptic neuron by stimulating small protein molecules located in the membrane of the postsynaptic neuron. These receptor molecules are the only part of the postsynaptic neuron that appear to be directly affected by contact with a transmitter substance.
4.17.	b, p. 97	In this situation, the only consequence for lever pressing is receipt of a small bit of electrical stimulation; no aversive stimulus is avoided and no electrical shock is delivered. The nervous system is partly electrical in nature, but that doesn't completely explain why rats will continue to lever press. Electrical stimulation of some parts of the brain causes rats to continue to lever press; electrical stimulation of other parts of the brain does not. This result suggests that some areas of the brain play a role in reward.
4.18.	d, p. 100	Without training (an environmental factor) Alison could not become an accomplished gymnast, even if she had superior genes for flexibility, balance, and muscle strength. And without genes that code for some minimal degree of these characteristics, all the training in the world would not help her to become an accomplished gymnast.
4.19.	b, p. 103	The right cerebral hemisphere controls activities of the left side of the body and the left cerebral hemisphere controls activities on the right side of the body. Thus, if Andy has damage to his right primary motor cortex, he will have difficulty executing movements on the left side of his body.
4.20.	d, p. 106	By definition, visual agnosia is the inability to recognize the identity or use of an object by means of vision. People with visual agnosia are not blind.
4.21.	d, p. 110	Postural adjustments are under the control of the cerebellum.
4.22.	d, p. 115	Drugs that affect the activity of acetylcholine-secreting neurons, such as curare, often cause respiratory problems, including suffocation.
4.23.	a, p. 117	Extensive use of cocaine and amphetamine produce symptoms of paranoid schizophrenia, including hallucinations.
4.24.	a, p. 119	Heroin, morphine, and opium, all of which are opiates, produce physiological dependence in the people who are addicted to them.

Practice Tests
CHAPTER 5: Practice Test 1

5.1. Short-term habituation
   a. is common in biologically simple organisms.
   b. depends on one's memory of previous experiences with the same stimulus.
   c. can be retained from day to day.
   d. has little, if any, adaptive value.

5.2. Any neutral stimulus paired with a stimulus such as food that elicits a response is called a(n) _____ stimulus.
   a. unconditional
   b. discriminative
   c. orienting
   d. conditional

5.3. After a response has been conditioned, what would happen if the UCS no longer followed the CS?
   a. The response would continue to occur much as it had before.
   b. The response would eventually be eliminated.
   c. The response would increase in strength.
   d. The response would first decrease in strength and then become stronger.

5.4. Leslie was in a car accident during a rain storm. Now whenever she must drive during the rain, even when it is only a sprinkle, she gets nervous. This response is likely due to
   a. discrimination.
   b. generalization.
   c. spontaneous recovery.
   d. extinction.

5.5. Classical conditioning will only occur when the
   a. subject's behavior is reinforced.
   b. CS reliably predicts the UCS.
   c. subject's reflexive behavior produces the CS.
   d. UCS reliably predicts the CS.

5.6. What is the function of the cumulative recorder?
   a. It records responses as they occur in time.
   b. It averages the number of responses made in each experimental session.
   c. It records all the activities of the organism under study in an operant experiment.
   d. all of the above

5.7. Any stimulus that follows a response and decreases the frequency of that response over time is called a
   a. positive reinforcer.
   b. negative reinforcer.
   c. punisher.
   d. discriminative stimulus.

5.8. The method of successive approximations relies on
   a. reinforcing the target behavior for successful shaping of novel behaviors.
   b. reinforcing each and every response that resembles the target behavior.
   c. gradually withholding more and more reinforcement over the course of an experimental session.
   d. reinforcing responses that increasingly resemble the target behavior.

5.9. One reason that human rituals originate and are maintained is that they
   a. are reinforced by the culture in which they are practiced.
   b. cause the occurrence of conditional stimuli.
   c. have superstitious properties.
   d. are part of our genetic endowment (and that is why rituals are universal in form and content).

5.10. Which of the following types of individuals is most likely to suffer from a flavor-aversion as a result of their medical treatment?
   a. a gall bladder patient
   b. a vasectomy patient
   c. a cancer patient
   d. a glaucoma patient

5.11. The emergence of novel behavior without the use of direct reinforcement is called
   a. rule-governed behavior.
   b. conditional responding.
   c. shaping.
   d. stimulus equivalence.

5.12. The early studies of insight learning suggested that
   a. it may involve a combination of classical conditioning and operant conditioning.
   b. reinforcement of certain behaviors is required for it to occur.
   c. it was not due to trial and error learning.
   d. learning a task and later performing it well requires practice.

Practice Tests
CHAPTER 5: Practice Test 2

5.13. In Pavlov's original research, the dogs only salivated to the sound of the tone if the
    a. tone followed the food powder.
    b. tone was extremely loud.
    c. food powder was presented soon after the tone.
    d. tone and the food powder were presented at the same time.

5.14. The finding that Siamese fighting fish are likely to win a fight if they are first given a warning regarding the presence of an intruder in their territory suggests that
    a. aggressive behavior is learned.
    b. even in fish, there is a "home-court" advantage.
    c. preparation is the key to winning aggressive encounters in the animal world.
    d. classical conditioning has important biological functions.

5.15. The reappearance of the CR in the next experimental session following a period of extinction is termed
    a. generalization.
    b. classical conditioning.
    c. discrimination.
    d. spontaneous recovery.

5.16. Several years ago you were bitten by a friend's dog. Since then you have been afraid of dogs and other animals that resemble dogs. Your reaction is an example of a(n)
    a. innate fear of animals that most people have.
    b. classically conditioned emotional response.
    c. irrational fear of pain.
    d. vivid memory of the dog's attack.

5.17. The main subjects in Thorndike's research were
    a. dogs that salivated.
    b. rats that escaped electric shock.
    c. pigeons that pecked lighted disks.
    d. cats that escaped puzzle boxes.

5.18. The discriminative stimulus gains strength as a result of
    a. its association with the consequences of behavior.
    b. becoming a conditional stimulus.
    c. the conditional responding that it controls.
    d. all of the above

5.19. The withholding of a reinforcing event causes the relevant behavior to
    a. increase.
    b. stay about the same.
    c. decrease to zero.
    d. decrease moderately.

5.20. The subjects in the Herrnstein and Loveland study (1964), _____, learned to respond to _____ through _____.
    a. rats; several similar tones; generalization training
    b. dogs; specific cats; discrimination training
    c. young children; the concept of animal; discrimination training
    d. pigeons; the concept of human beings; discrimination training

5.21. Garcia and Koelling's research on flavor-aversion learning demonstrated that
   a. conditioning can occur to almost any CS.
   b. certain CSs are better predictors of certain UCSs than are other CSs.
   c. flavor-aversion learning is most effective when the delay between the CS and UCS is over 24 hours.
   d. flavor-aversions are sometimes formed by cancer patients while undergoing certain forms of chemotherapy.

5.22. Imitation learning
   a. occurs only in humans.
   b. is the quickest form of learning.
   c. requires only one CS-UCS pairing.
   d. is learning through observation.

5.23. An important discovery in the field of behavioral pharmacology is that
   a. most psychoactive drugs can function as reinforcers.
   b. psychoactive drugs are addictive.
   c. psychoactive drugs may be abused.
   d. drug-taking behavior is due primarily to cognitive factors.

5.24. Behavior analysts and cognitive psychologists agree that
   a. thoughts can cause behavior.
   b. thoughts exist and thinking is important.
   c. operant behavior has cognitive components.
   d. the capacity to form mental representations of the environment is the basis for learning.

Practice Test Answers
CHAPTER 5: Practice Test 1

5.1.   a, p. 126   Animals with simple nervous systems are capable of showing only simple forms of learning, such as short-term habituation.

5.2.   d, p. 128   By definition, the conditional stimulus is any neutral stimulus, which, through its pairing with an appetitive stimulus, elicits a conditional response.

5.3.   b, p. 130   In most cases where the UCS no longer follows the CS, extinction of the CR results.

5.4.   b, p. 131   Many conditional responses, including emotional responses, generalize to stimuli that resemble the original CS. In this case, rainy conditions, because they resemble the conditions of Leslie's accident, make Leslie nervous.

5.5.   b, p. 133   In circumstances in which the CS does not regularly predict the occurrence of the UCS, classical conditioning of responding does not occur. Thus, appearance of the CS just before the occurrence of the UCS is a necessary factor for classical conditioning to develop.

5.6.   a, p. 135   The cumulative recorder is a device that records responses as they occur in time (see Figure 5.8 on page 135).

5.7.   c, p. 137   By definition, a punisher is any stimulus that is contingent on responding and reduces the frequency of that response in the future.

5.8.   d, p. 139   The method of successive approximations involves reinforcing responses that, over time, increasingly resemble the desired response.

5.9.   a, p. 145   The communities in which we live differentially reward us through social approval for following the cultural practices and customs they deem important. Many differences in cultures can be traced to the particular values that cultures placed on different behaviors.

5.10. c, p. 150   An important finding in medical research is that chemotherapy induces flavor-aversions in cancer patients. The last food eaten prior to chemotherapy is most often the object of the aversion.

5.11. d, p. 152   By definition, stimulus equivalence is the emergence of novel behavior without direct reinforcement of that behavior.

5.12. c, p. 154   The earliest studies of insight concluded that this form of learning appeared spontaneously, without experience and without making mistakes (as in trial and error learning).

Practice Test Answers
CHAPTER 5: Practice Test 2

5.13. c, p. 127 Pavlov was the first researcher to demonstrate the importance of the timing of the CS-UCS pairing in classical conditioning. Specifically, most forms of classical conditioning require that the UCS immediately follow the appearance of the CS (later studies showed that the optimal timing was 0.5 seconds).

5.14. d, p. 129 In this case, fish that were given a warning signal (the CS) were better at defending their territories against an intruder (the UCS) than were fish that were not given a warning signal.

5.15. d, p. 131 By definition, spontaneous recovery is the reappearance of a response that has been previously extinguished. The reappearance of the response usually occurs after a period of time has elapsed since it was extinguished.

5.16. b, p. 131 Many fears and other types of emotional responding are the result of a pairing of a stimulus (CS), such as a dog, with an aversive event (the UCS), such as being bitten by a dog.

5.17. d, p. 134 Thorndike's experimental research on the law of effect involved placing cats in a "puzzle box" and recording the amount of time they required to escape from it.

5.18. a, p. 136 As Figure 5.9 on page 136 shows, the consequences of responding strengthen the ability of the discriminative stimulus to set the occasion for the response that produces those consequences.

5.19. c, p. 138 In operant conditioning, the withholding of a reinforcer causes the behavior that would normally produce that reinforcer to extinguish.

5.20. d, p. 142 The subjects in this study, pigeons, were shown slides, some of which featured human beings. The birds were given a bit of food when they pecked a plastic disk following the presentation of a slide featuring a human being. They were not given any food for pecking the disk following the presentation of a slide not featuring a human being. They soon learned to peck at the disk only following the presentation of the slides showing humans.

5.21. b, p. 148 In this study, the animals learned that illness was predicted by flavor and that shock was predicted by lights and sounds. The animals showed no avoidance of drinking when exposure to lights and sounds preceded illness or when shock was preceded by a particular flavor.

5.22. d, p. 151 Only by observing another engaging in a behavior can we imitate that behavior.

5.23. a, p. 152 Drugs that reinforce behavior are those that are most likely to be addictive. Many drugs are now routinely tested for their reinforcing properties in an effort to predict which ones are likely to be addictive.

5.24. b, p. 156 Although behavior analysts and cognitive psychologists disagree over the causal nature of thoughts and other internal, private events, they agree that thoughts exist and that they are important aspects of everyday life.

Practice Tests
CHAPTER 6: Practice Test 1

6.1. A neuron that responds directly to physical energy is called a _____ cell.
   a. receptor
   b. transducer
   c. sense organ
   d. Weber

6.2. Which of the following qualifies as a false alarm?
   a. A signal is absent and the subject responds "no."
   b. A signal is absent and the subject responds "yes."
   c. A signal is present and the subject responds "no."
   d. A signal is present and the subject responds "yes."

6.3. The space immediately behind the _____ is filled with a fluid called _____.
   a. cornea; aqueous humor
   b. sclera; vitreous humor
   c. retina; aqueous humor
   d. optic nerve; vitreous humor

6.4. The key vitamin involved in the transduction of radiant energy is vitamin
   a. A.
   b. B.
   c. D.
   d. E.

6.5. In terms of color vision, which of the following does NOT belong with the other three?
   a. humans
   b. dogs
   c. birds
   d. fish

6.6. Yellow light stimulates which photoreceptor(s)?
   a. yellow
   b. blue and green
   c. red and blue
   d. red and green

6.7. Downward flexing of the basilar membrane causes the _____ to bulge outward.
   a. oval window
   b. cochlea
   c. round window
   d. ear drum

6.8. White noise contains
   a. primarily sounds of less than 200 Hz.
   b. sounds above 20,000 Hz.
   c. no sounds of an audible frequency.
   d. all frequencies of sound.

6.9. Which kind of sound is the most effective at causing large solid objects to vibrate?
   a. low frequency sounds
   b. medium frequency sounds
   c. medium to high frequency sounds
   d. high frequency sounds

6.10. Another term for the "bumps" on the tongue is
   a. papillae.
   b. taste buds.
   c. taste receptors.
   d. microvilli.

6.11. Among humans, olfaction plays an important role in
   a. identifying each other.
   b. attracting potential mates.
   c. identifying spoiled food.
   d. repelling people we don't like.

6.12. Our receptors for temperature respond best to _____ temperature.
   a. low
   b. high
   c. constant
   d. changes in

Practice Tests
CHAPTER 6: Practice Test 2

6.13. The study of the quantitative relation between physical stimuli and perceptual experience is known as
   a. signal detection.
   b. sensory psychology.
   c. psychophysics.
   d. perceptual psychology.

6.14. According to the text, which of the following explanations is NOT likely to explain the positive testimonials given by users of subliminal self-help tapes?
   a. The effort to achieve one's goal is justified by the perception of positive results.
   b. A person's expectations make achieving his or her goal more likely.
   c. Buying these kind of tapes suggests that the person has an interest in self-improvement.
   d. The tapes cause improvement by producing visible changes in the person's behavior through learning.

6.15. Visual information follows which of the following routes to the brain?
   a. ganglion cells, bipolar cells, photoreceptors
   b. photoreceptors, ganglion cells, bipolar cells
   c. photoreceptors, bipolar cells, ganglion cells
   d. bipolar cells, ganglion cells, photoreceptors

6.16. Which kinds of eye movements ensures that the image of an object will fall on corresponding portions of each retina?
   a. conjugate movements
   b. saccadic movements
   c. rotary movements
   d. pursuit movements

6.17. The addition of two or more lights of different wavelengths is called _____ mixing.
   a. pigment
   b. wavelength
   c. color
   d. hue

6.18. An alternating pattern of high and low air pressure is known as
   a. a sound wave.
   b. the amplitude of a sound wave.
   c. the timbre of a sound wave.
   d. the complexity of a sound wave.

6.19. A perfectly healthy ear can hear frequencies of about _____ Hz.
   a. 20,000
   b. 30,000
   c. 40,000
   d. 50,000

6.20.	The lowest, and usually most intense, frequency of a complex sound is called
   a. timbre.
   b. the fundamental frequency.
   c. an overtone.
   d. pitch.

6.21.	The primary members of the Deaf community are those who
   a. are postlingually deaf.
   b. are prelingually deaf.
   c. use sign language.
   d. have received educational training in oral communication.

6.22.	One of the places in the brain that olfactory information is sent to is the _____, which plays a role in both _____.
   a. limbic system; emotion and memory
   b. hypothalamus; homeostasis and thirst
   c. amygdala; emotion and aggression
   d. cerebellum; movement and coordination

6.23.	Which of the following is NOT one of the somatosenses?
   a. changes in laterality
   b. pain
   c. touch
   d. vibration

6.24.	Skin sensitivity may be determined using the
   a. method of limits.
   b. signal detection method.
   c. two-point threshold method.
   d. method of constant stimuli.

Practice Test Answers
CHAPTER 6: Practice Test 1

6.1. a, p. 162 By definition, a receptor cell is a neuron that responds directly to physical stimulation.

6.2. b, p. 165 By definition, a false alarm occurs when a subject in a signal detection study reports that a stimulus is present when, in fact, it is not.

6.3. a, p. 170 As Figure 6.8 on page 170 shows, the area behind the cornea is filled with aqueous humor.

6.4. a, p. 173 A molecule that is derived from vitamin A is the key chemical agent involved in the transduction of light.

6.5. b, p. 175 Among the species listed as possible answers to this question, only dogs do not have color vision.

6.6. d, p. 177 The subjective experience of seeing the color yellow occurs only when red and green cones are stimulated.

6.7. c, p. 182 Downward movement of the basilar membrane displaces the fluid of the inner ears, which causes the round window to bulge outward.

6.8. d, p. 185 White noise is the combination of all frequencies of sound.

6.9. a, p. 186 Large solid objects vibrate only in response to low-frequency sounds (and for this reason, they are excellent at masking high-frequency sounds).

6.10. a, p. 190 By definition, papillae are the bumps found on the tongue.

6.11. c, p. 191 Although we do not have the olfactory sensitivity that many other animals do, we are able to detect the odors of foods that may be dangerous for us to eat, especially foods that have spoiled.

6.12. d, p. 194 Many of our "skin receptors," including those for temperature, respond optimally to changes in stimulation and respond least to constant, non-changing stimulation.

Practice Test Answers
CHAPTER 6: Practice Test 2

6.13. c, p. 163 By definition, psychophysics is the study of the quantitative relation between physical stimuli and our perceptual experience.

6.14. d, p. 167 Subliminal tapes do not appear to exert much, if any, influence directly on our behavior. Instead, they seem more likely to influence our perception of any changes in our behavior and our attributing these changes to the tapes themselves.

6.15. c, p. 171 On its way to the brain, visual information is sent from the photoreceptor to the bipolar cells. From there, it is sent to the ganglion cells and then to the brain.

6.16. a, p. 174 The function of conjugate movements is to keep both eyes fixed on a target. In other words, these movements keep the image of the target fixed on corresponding portions of each retina.

6.17. c, p. 176 By definition, color mixing is the mixing of two or more lights of different wavelengths.

6.18. a, p. 181 By definition, a sound wave is an alternating pattern of high and low air pressure.

6.19. a, p. 183 When a healthy human ear is tested for sensitivity to different sound frequencies, researchers have learned that it can hear frequencies as high as 20,000 Hz.

6.20. b, p. 186 By definition, the fundamental frequency is the lowest and generally most intense frequency of a complex sound.

6.21. c, p. 187 The members of the Deaf community tend to be those person who have learned to use sign language as their primary means of communication.

6.22. a, p. 191 Olfactory information is sent to the limbic system, which is a brain center involved in both memory and emotion. One reason that we may recall a person, place, or thing when we smell a familiar odor is probably because the limbic system is where olfactory information is received by the brain.

6.23. a, p. 193 Our somatosenses are unable to detect changes laterality; our somatosenses are able to detect pain, touch, and vibration.

6.24. c, p. 194 A very common means of detecting skin sensitivity to stimulation is the two-point threshold.

Practice Tests
CHAPTER 7: Practice Test 1

7.1. The act of perceiving
    a. actually involves two steps, sensing and perceiving.
    b. is rapid, automatic, and unconscious.
    c. occurs primarily in mammals.
    d. involves considerable planning and forethought.

7.2. Information contained in the mosaic of the primary visual cortex is rendered interpretable
    a. in the prefrontal association cortex.
    b. in the motor association area of the cortex.
    c. at the edge of the primary visual cortex.
    d. in the visual association cortex.

7.3. The inability to tell the difference among different hues is called
    a. aphasia.
    b. apraxia.
    c. agnosia.
    d. achromatopsia.

7.4. Gestalt psychologists would argue that what we see is actually a product of
    a. the nature of the stimulus elements that we perceive.
    b. relationships among elements of the stimulus.
    c. the nature of the background behind the object we are viewing.
    d. our psyche.

7.5. Most psychologists view the template model as
    a. being an appropriate model of common fate.
    b. a reasonable explanation for feature detection.
    c. being an unworkable model.
    d. a more accurate model of pattern recognition than the prototype model.

7.6. One shortcoming of the distinctive features model is that it cannot account for the
    a. fact people that can sometimes recognize complex stimuli faster than they can simpler stimuli.
    b. excessively large amount of time that people take to recognize large stimuli.
    c. finding that people easily recognize stimuli that are different from other stimuli.
    d. finding that humans are the only organism that appears to use prototypes in pattern recognition.

7.7. With respect to the geon hypothesis, it seems MOST likely that geons are involved in the perception of
    a. specific objects.
    b. geometric patterns.
    c. prototypes of generic classes of objects.
    d. any object formed by a geon or a combination of geons.

7.8. A _____ is a computing device that performs several operations simultaneously.
    a. serial processor
    b. central processing unit
    c. parallel processor
    d. analog processor

7.9. Bottom-up processing is to _____ as top-down processing is to _____.
  a. visual perception; pattern recognition
  b. data driven; context driven
  c. parallel processing; serial processing
  d. context driven; data driven

7.10. An object will appear closer if its surface is
  a. smooth.
  b. coarse.
  c. convergent.
  d. partially blocked by another object.

7.11. As we move past a visual scene, objects closer to us appear to pass in front of objects farther away. This depth cue is called
  a. convergence.
  b. linear perspective.
  c. motion parallax.
  d. elevation.

7.12. Form constancy may be demonstrated by
  a. decreasing the size of the retinal image.
  b. increasing the size of the retinal image.
  c. decreasing the distance from the object.
  d. an unchanging perception of objects in terms of their size and shape.

Practice Tests
CHAPTER 7: Practice Test 2

7.13. The optic nerves send visual information to the _____ , which, in turn, sends it to the _____.
   a. limbic system; occipital lobe
   b. thalamus; primary visual cortex
   c. hypothalamus; primary visual cortex
   d. cingulate gyrus; occipital cortex

7.14. Which of the following areas is responsible for the perception of three-dimensional forms?
   a. the first level of the association cortex in the occipital lobe
   b. the second level of the association cortex in the parietal lobe
   c. the second level of the association cortex in the temporal lobe
   d. the primary visual cortex

7.15. Suppose that I have sustained damage to my visual association cortex. Also suppose that I am a dog breeder who, after my accident, can no longer tell my dogs apart. You correctly surmise that the brain damage is causing me to suffer from
   a. achromatopsia.
   b. Balint's syndrome.
   c. visual agnosia.
   d. prosopagnosia.

7.16. From a distance a "C" may appear to be an "O." This is an example of which Gestalt law?
   a. proximity
   b. closure
   c. good continuation
   d. similarity

7.17. Evidence that the human visual system may store many prototypes derives from a study that showed that people
   a. shown thousands of color slides recognized most of them weeks later.
   b. have at least two prototypes for each object they encounter.
   c. have a single prototype for each object they encounter.
   d. often have some difficulty in recognizing new faces.

7.18. Biederman proposes that there are _____ different geons.
   a. 12
   b. 26
   c. 32
   d. 36

7.19. A major advantage to computer modeling is that
   a. computers can be programmed to think independent of the computer program.
   b. computers are getting easier for most people to understand.
   c. computers are able to represent every aspect of human thought.
   d. computers are able to think concretely about a complex process.

7.20. Visual perception appears to consist of _____, each of which involves a different _____.
   a. several forms of pattern recognition; geon
   b. a series of analyses; neural network
   c. three distinct levels of computation; parallel processor
   d. a hierarchy of prototypes; geon

7.21. When viewing nearby objects, the angle between the eyes is _____ when viewing distant objects.
   a. larger than
   b. much smaller than
   c. about the same size as
   d. slightly smaller than

7.22. As I look out of my office window, I can make out the details of nearby objects very easily. As I look at objects farther away, I have a more difficult time in making out the details of different objects. This example describes the cue to depth called
   a. linear perspective.
   b. texture.
   c. shading.
   d. interposition.

7.23. The notion that a culture's language reflects the thoughts and perceptions of its members is called the _____ principle.
   a. linguistic relativity
   b. universal language
   c. speech-thought
   d. language structure

7.24. The detection of movement is
   a. more learned than genetic.
   b. secondary to the perception of fine detail.
   c. one of the most primitive aspects of vision.
   d. a recently evolved visual characteristic.

Practice Test Answers
CHAPTER 7: Practice Test 1

7.1.   b, p. 201   Our perception of the world around us requires no conscious effort on our behalf and occurs instantly during our waking hours.

7.2.   d, p. 202   Researchers have established that the information we receive from our visual fields corresponds to specific modules of the primary visual cortex. The information contained in these modules is then combined in the visual association cortex.

7.3.   d, p. 204   By definition, achromatopsia is the inability to discriminate among different hues.

7.4.   b, p. 207   One of Gestalt's contributions to psychology was its argument that the perception of any stimulus involves "seeing" the relationship among the elements that make up the stimulus.

7.5.   c, p. 208   The template model of pattern perception is seen by most psychologists as being a simple but impractical model because it would require people to store and be able to use a seemingly infinite number of templates for seeing and recognizing objects. Other models have the virtue of being more representative of the manner in which the visual system actually works.

7.6.   a, p. 210   Often the additional cues provided by complex stimuli make it easier to recognize these stimuli than to recognize simpler stimuli that have fewer cues.

7.7.   c, p. 211   Geons seem unlikely to represent specific objects; that would require having a geon for each and every different object that we encounter! Instead, Biederman and others propose that geons are more like prototypes of classes of objects, which means that we would require far fewer of them to recognize most objects.

7.8.   c, p. 213   By definition, a parallel processor is a computing device that can perform several operations simultaneously.

7.9.   b, p. 215   Bottom-up processing involves using elements of the stimulus to drive the perceptual process whereas top-down processing uses elements of the context in which the stimulus is presented to drive the perceptual process.

7.10.   b, p. 219   The monocular cue called texture allows us to judge depth based on the fineness or coarseness of an object's surface; objects with coarser textures appear closer.

7.11.   c, p. 221   By definition, motion parallax involves the apparent movement of closer objects; more distant objects appear to remain fixed or to move more slowly relative to closer objects.

7.12.   d, p. 225   By definition, form constancy means that our perceptions of objects do not change in terms of size and shape as their images on our retinas change position and shape.

Practice Test Answers
CHAPTER 7: Practice Test 2

7.13.   b, p. 201   Once visual information leaves the retina, it first goes to the thalamus and then to the visual cortex.

7.14.   c, p. 203   Studies involving patients with brain damage and studies involving PET scans have shown that the second level of the association cortex in the temporal lobe is involved in the perception of three-dimensional objects.

7.15.   d, p. 205   Studies involving brain damaged people have revealed that prosopagnosia is caused by damage to the visual association cortex.

7.16.   b, p. 208   The Gestalt law of closure holds that any elements missing from an outline of a figure will be "filled-in" by our visual system. Thus, a "C" may be perceived to be an "O."

7.17.   a, p. 209   Standing's (1973) study, in which people were shown over 10,000 slides, demonstrated that people could still recognize most of them despite having seen them only once several weeks earlier. This finding suggests that people use prototypes rather than templates to recognize objects; it would seem unlikely that people would have created and stored a separate template for each slide.

7.18.   d, p. 211   Biederman has, in fact, suggested that there are 36 different geons that are combined to create all of the different objects in our environments.

7.19.   d, p. 212   Computers can be used to represent a very formal, concrete process of thought, even in regard to the most complex processes. If a process can be broken down into its constituent parts, then a computer can probably be programmed to "think" about that process.

7.20.   b, p. 214   Recent conceptions of visual perception hold that visual perception involves a series of analyses, each involving a different neural network, beginning with very simple features, and then progressing to more complex ones.

7.21.   a, p. 218   As Figure 7.26 on page 218 illustrates, when the eyes converge on a close object the angle between them is greater than when they converge on a more distant object.

7.22.   b, p. 219   The monocular cue called texture allows us to perceive depth according to the fineness or coarseness of the objects we are viewing. Objects that are close to us appear coarse and we can clearly see their fine details. More distant objects appear smoother and we are able to see fewer of their details.

7.23.   a, p. 223   By definition, the linguistic relativity principle holds that the language a culture speaks reflects that culture's thoughts and perceptions.

7.24.   c, p. 225   Even animals with very primitive visual systems are able to detect the movement of objects in their environments.

Practice Tests
CHAPTER 8: Practice Test 1

8.1. Which of the following is NOT a cognitive process involved in memory?
   a. perceiving
   b. encoding
   c. storage
   d. retrieval

8.2. Information can enter short-term memory
   a. from iconic memory only.
   b. from long-term memory only.
   c. from both iconic and long-term memory.
   d. only if it is rehearsed.

8.3. Which of the following statements is FALSE?
   a. Chunking is a form of encoding information.
   b. A chunk contains 7 +/-2 items.
   c. Chunking creates meaningful units of information.
   d. Chunking may be accomplished through the use of rules.

8.4. Conduction aphasia is caused by brain damage that
   a. destroys the ability to consolidate information in an unbiased manner.
   b. disrupts connections between Wernicke's and Broca's areas.
   c. produces short-term retrograde amnesia.
   d. inhibits the neural circuits that constitute working memory.

8.5. Some of the strongest evidence for the consolidation hypothesis stems from
   a. Peterson and Peterson's research.
   b. disruption of normal brain functioning.
   c. Shepard and Metzler's research.
   d. enhancement of brain functioning involving people who have been trained to use mnemonic devices.

8.6. Shallow processing is to _____ features as deep processing is to _____ features.
   a. semantic; meaningful
   b. contextual; elaborative
   c. superficial; meaningful
   d. physical; surface

8.7. The idea that how we encode information may affect our ability to later retrieve it is termed
   a. semantic encoding.
   b. encoding specificity.
   c. procedural encoding.
   d. encoding salience.

8.8. According to Sachs's research, the _____ of a sentence is remembered better than the _____ of a sentence.
   a. form; meaning
   b. meaning; form
   c. beginning; ending
   d. ending; beginning

8.9. Information regarding which of the following is NOT likely to be stored in implicit memory?
   a. the time of day
   b. playing the piano
   c. catching a football
   d. driving a car

8.10. Even a carefully conducted experiment on animals is unlikely to yield valuable information about _____ memory.
   a. episodic
   b. semantic
   c. autobiographical
   d. all of the above

8.11. The usefulness of any retrieval cue is influenced by
   a. the length of the list of words to be remembered.
   b. the personality of the person who is trying to remember something.
   c. the experience of the person who is trying to remember something.
   d. encoding specificity.

8.12. Bartlett's research indicated that
   a. people tend to remember the main idea of most stories.
   b. the remembering of any story is very specific to the events in the story.
   c. people tend to reconstruct missing portions of a story based on their expectations.
   d. remembering the details of a story is easier than remembering the details of major historical events.

Practice Tests
CHAPTER 8: Practice Test 2

8.13. In Sperling's research, the tone that was delayed for more than one second had the effect of _____ subjects' ability to recall the material.
   a. improving
   b. hampering
   c. at first improving and then hampering
   d. at first hampering and then improving

8.14. If not rehearsed, information stays in short-term memory for less than _____ seconds.
   a. 5
   b. 10
   c. 15
   d. 20

8.15. According to Baddeley, which of the following plays a role in phonological working memory?
   a. articulatory and visual coding
   b. auditory and articulatory coding
   c. acoustic and verbal coding
   d. auditory and acoustic coding

8.16. Which of the following appears to be the most important cause of loss of information from short-term memory?
   a. decay
   b. forgetting
   c. displacement
   d. fading

8.17. Craik and Tulving's research suggests that complex sentences
   a. provide more information than less complex sentences, which leads to better retention of that information.
   b. provide more information than less complex sentences, which leads to less distinctive memories.
   c. are more difficult to recall than simple ones.
   d. do not produce adequate mental imagery for the precise recall of complex information.

8.18. Automatic processing is to _____ as effortful processing is to _____.
   a. easy; difficult
   b. remembering the name of a close friend; textbook learning
   c. frequency, place, and time; shallow and deep processing
   d. all of the above

8.19. The key to the effectiveness of any mnemonic system is that it
   a. simplifies the information to be remembered.
   b. decreases the amount of total information to be stored.
   c. makes use of information already stored in memory.
   d. all of the above

8.20. Conceptual information is stored in _____ memory.
   a. semantic
   b. episodic
   c. inherent
   d. working

8.21. Arlo has a big exam in psychology coming up next week. Based on what you know about retrieval cues, you correctly advise him to
   a. read each chapter thoroughly.
   b. study all of the key terms and concepts in each of the chapters.
   c. do as much effortful processing as possible.
   d. study for the exam in the classroom in which he will take the exam.

8.22. Damage to the hippocampus may affect neural activity by affecting
   a. the release of transmitter substances.
   b. synaptic connections.
   c. the production of transmitter substances.
   d. all of the above

8.23. The tip-of-the-tongue phenomenon
   a. occurs about twice a week.
   b. is more frequent among younger people than older people.
   c. often involves adjectives and adverbs.
   d. is solved about half of the time.

8.24. When is interference with retrieval most likely?
   a. after periods of sleep
   b. after periods of wakefulness
   c. during periods of drowsiness
   d. all of the above

Practice Test Answers
CHAPTER 8: Practice Test 1

8.1.   a, p. 232   Memory involves only three fundamental processes: the encoding, storage, and retrieval of information.

8.2.   c, p. 236   New information enters short-term memory from sensory memory. However, old information, used to interpret or otherwise process that information, enters short-term memory from long-term memory.

8.3.   b, p. 238   A chunk is a manageable, simplified bit of information. A chunk can be as small as a single letter or number or it can be as large as a string of letters and numbers. Short-term memory can hold approximately 7+/-2 chunks of information.

8.4.   b, p. 239   Research evidence suggests that disrupting the neural connections between Wernicke's and Broca's areas produces conduction aphasia, or the inability to remember words that are heard.

8.5.   b, p. 243   In general, people have known for a long time that a blow to the head can cause memory problems for recent events. This general observation has led people to speculate that a blow to the head interferes with the consolidation of memory as information is being transferred from short-term memory to long-term memory.

8.6.   c, p. 245   By definition, shallow processing involves the analysis of superficial characteristics of stimuli, and deep processing involves the analysis of the more complex and meaningful characteristics of a stimulus.

8.7.   b, p. 246   By definition, the encoding specificity principle holds that how we encode information affects our ability to retrieve it later.

8.8.   b, p. 250   An important finding in Sachs's research is that people tend to focus on the meaning of a sentence more than they do the form of it. As a result, they can remember more about the sentence's meaning than they can its form.

8.9.   a, p. 252   Implicit memory is memory of which a person is unaware. Thus, we are often not aware of the exact time that certain events took place, but we are aware of memories related to playing a musical instrument or a sport and to the performance of many acts, such as driving a car.

8.10.   b, p. 255   Semantic memory deals with the meaning of verbal information. Because animals do not possess a capacity for spoken language, they are unlikely to possess semantic memory.

8.11.   d, p. 258   The principle of encoding specificity holds that how we encode information will influence our ability to recall it later. Most cues that people use to remember information are present when information is first encoded.

8.12.   c, p. 261   Bartlett's early research on memory showed that people remember only a few important details about a story and tend to reconstruct the story from memory by filling in the details according to their expectations regarding the events of story.

Practice Test Answers
CHAPTER 8: Practice Test 2

8.13. b, p. 234 Sperling's research on sensory memory revealed the fragile nature of iconic memory. In particular, one important finding from his research was that iconic memory holds information for very brief durations. Delaying recall as little as one second had the effect of hampering people's recall by as much as fifty percent.

8.14. d, p. 237 Peterson and Peterson's research involving the distractor task in a study of short-term memory showed that unrehearsed information stays in short-term memory for 20 seconds or less.

8.15. b, p. 239 Baddeley's research suggested that both auditory and articulatory coding may play a role in phonological working memory.

8.16. c, p. 241 Because of the limited capacity of short-term memory (7+/-2 items), displacement appears to be the most important cause of loss of information in short-term information. Information is simply jettisoned to make more room for new information.

8.17. a, p. 245 Craik and Tulving's (1975) research suggests that people will remember information better if it is meaningful (and thus more complex) than information that is simple.

8.18. d, p. 246 Automatic processing of information is effortless and operates in very familiar contexts such as remembering the name of a close friend. Automatic processing is also affected by the frequency with which we are exposed to information as well contextual variables such as the place and time in which events occur. Effortful processing is more difficult and is involved in learning complex information such as that found in text books. Effortful processing involves both shallow and deep forms of processing.

8.19. c, p. 247 All mnemonic systems make use of information already stored in memory. For example, the method of loci is based on geographic information, such as the landmarks along your walk or ride to school, of which you are already aware.

8.20. a, p. 251 By definition, semantic memory is memory for facts, data, and vocabulary.

8.21. d, p. 259 According to the principle of encoding specificity, the best way to remember information is to establish strong retrieval cues when that information is first encoded. Our recall for information will thus be best when we attempt to recall under conditions similar to those present during encoding.

8.22. d, p. 256 Damage to the hippocampus interferes with the synaptic activities that occur there. Thus, if memories are formed by changes in the neural activity in the hippocampus, memory will be disrupted by synaptic changes, including the production and release of transmitter substances.

8.23. d, p. 257 Researchers who have studied the tip-of-the-tongue phenomenon have found that it occurs about once a week, increases with age, involves proper nouns and knowing the first letter of the word, and it is solved correctly about half the time.

8.24. b, p. 263 Because new memories are formed while we are awake, interference problems in retrieval are more likely to occur after periods of wakefulness.

Practice Tests
CHAPTER 9: Practice Test 1

9.1. Self-awareness appears to be the result of our
    a. ability to communicate.
    b. consciousness.
    c. social nature.
    d. sense of self.

9.2. Implicit memories provide evidence that
    a. unattended information is generally lost.
    b. attended information that is not meaningful is generally lost.
    c. unattended information may be remembered.
    d. selective attention is necessary for all forms of memory.

9.3. Rock and Gutman's study involved people being shown overlapping shapes of different colors. They were instructed to pay attention to only one of the colors. Later, in a recognition test, these people recognized
    a. both the attended and non-attended shapes.
    b. only those shapes that were pictured in the subject's favorite color.
    c. only the attended shape.
    d. very few of the attended or non-attended shapes.

9.4. Techniques for withdrawing attention or for dishabituating consciousness have in common the fact that they both
    a. stress the importance of encountering novel stimuli.
    b. involve chanting or focusing on a specific objects.
    c. are used to increase selective attention.
    d. have the same goal: to produce a change in consciousness.

9.5. For people with healthy brains, the two cerebral hemispheres
    a. function independently of each other.
    b. collaborate to process and integrate information.
    c. overlap considerably in their functions.
    d. integrate information except for highly specialized functions.

9.6. The person who discovered hypnosis was
    a. Freud.
    b. Breuer.
    c. Hilgard.
    d. Mesmer.

9.7. Hypnosis is a
    a. special case of learning.
    b. restructuring of perceptual-cognitive functioning.
    c. form of goal directed behavior.
    d. none of the above

9.8. An important implication of Milgram's study on hypnosis was that
   a. under hypnosis some people are likely to commit antisocial acts.
   b. control groups are necessary in hypnosis research that is aimed at determining whether people will commit antisocial acts while under hypnosis.
   c. hypnotic suggestions are maximally effective on people who have vivid imaginations.
   d. a key factor in the effectiveness of hypnosis is the extent to which the person being hypnotized trusts the hypnotist.

9.9. The apparatus that is used to measure the electrical activity of the heart is called an
   a. electro-oculogram.
   b. electromyogram.
   c. electroencephalogram.
   d. electrocardiogram.

9.10. How many stages of sleep are there (including REM sleep)?
   a. 4
   b. 5
   c. 6
   d. 8

9.11. If you woke me during _____ sleep, I could tell you all about any dream that I was having at that time.
   a. stage 3
   b. slow-wave
   c. REM
   d. stage 1 or 2

9.12. The basic rest activity cycle (BRAC) is a _____-minute cycle in alternating levels of alertness controlled by the _____; during sleep it controls cycles of _____.
   a. 90; pons; REM sleep and slow-wave sleep
   b. 60; medulla; REM sleep
   c. 45; raphe nucleus; slow-wave sleep
   d. 30; brain stem; REM and slow-wave sleep

Practice Tests
CHAPTER 9: Practice Test 2

9.13. Most forms of communication among non-human animals are
   a. conscious.
   b. symbolic expression of private events.
   c. learned and therefore entail some form of consciousness.
   d. automatic responses and do not involve consciousness.

9.14. In a dichotic listening task, information that is channeled into the unattended ear is
   a. able to enter a person's consciousness.
   b. able to influence behavior.
   c. placed in some sort of temporary storage system.
   d. all of the above

9.15. The one function that all methods of altering consciousness have in common is to produce a change in
   a. attention.
   b. metabolism.
   c. meditation.
   d. physical activity.

9.16. The inability to recognize the identity of an object visually is called visual
   a. aphasia.
   b. apraxia.
   c. amnesia.
   d. agnosia.

9.17. When information is presented to the left visual field, a person with split-brain syndrome is unable to respond verbally to it because the
   a. person is unable to perceive the information.
   b. person does not perceive the information accurately.
   c. information cannot be relayed to the language area of the brain.
   d. information is lost in memory before the person can verbalize a description of it.

9.18. Failure to remember what occurred during hypnosis as induced by suggestions made by the hypnotist is called posthypnotic
   a. forgetting.
   b. interference.
   c. retrieval failure.
   d. amnesia.

9.19. The dependent variable in Orne's study of hypnotized subjects was whether
   a. subjects' dominant hands would become rigid.
   b. subjects would get out of their chairs and start dancing.
   c. subjects would be susceptible to the Ponzo illusion.
   d. subjects' behaviors would conform to the hypnotist's suggestion to growl like a tiger.

9.20. The apparatus that is used to measure the electrical activity of the brain is called an
   a. electro-oculogram.
   b. electromyogram.
   c. electroencephalogram.
   d. electrocardiogram.

9.21. During stage 3 and stage 4 sleep, EEG recordings of the brain's electrical activity generally show _____ activity.
a. alpha
b. beta
c. theta
d. delta

9.22. Sleep deprivation has been found to interfere with
a. the ability to perform physical tasks.
b. the ability to react to stressful situations.
c. language abilities.
d. the ability to perform tasks that require vigilance.

9.23. Recent psychological research suggests that we dream because
a. dreams are one of the mind's ways of coping with stressful life events.
b. dreams release unused psychological energy at the day's end.
c. dreams are necessary to provide the brain with stimulation while it rests.
d. none of the above

9.24. Which of the following is NOT a disorder associated with slow-wave sleep?
a. enuresis
b. sleepwalking
c. night terrors
d. cataplexy

Practice Test Answers
CHAPTER 9: Practice Test 1

9.1.　a, p. 272　Our ability to use language allows us to communicate with others. Through this process we become aware of, and describe, our feelings and thoughts. Without this ability such self-awareness may not be possible.

9.2.　c, p. 273　Implicit memories do not require that we consciously attend to information to remember it. Thus, not all the information that we fail to attend to is lost.

9.3.　c, p. 278　Focusing attention on environmental stimuli strengthens the possibility that we will remember it later. Subjects in the Rock and Gutman (1981) study did not remember the stimuli to which they did not attend; they remembered only the stimuli to which they had attended.

9.4.　d, p. 279　Whether a meditation exercise causes people to attend more closely to a stimulus or to withdraw attention from a stimulus, the function is to produce a change in one's state of consciousness.

9.5.　b, p. 283　Each hemisphere of the brain transfers information back and forth by means of the corpus callosum, a bundle of neurons that connects the two hemispheres. Without the corpus callosum, a person would have, in effect, two brains. In this condition, information is not well integrated.

9.6.　d, p. 285　History gives credit for the discovery of hypnotism to Franz Anton Mesmer, an Austrian physician who passed magnets back and forth over people's bodies. The patients did not respond to the magnets so much as they did to Mesmer's suggestions.

9.7.　d, p. 286　Hypnosis involves a change of consciousness; it is not a form of learning, a restructuring of cognitive-perceptual function, nor a form of goal directed behavior.

9.8.　b, p. 289　Control groups are necessary in research on hypnosis because hypnotized subjects might perform a behavior even if they were not hypnotized. Milgram's study pointed out the usefulness of control groups in hypnotic research.

9.9.　d, p. 290　By definition, an electrocardiogram records the electrical activity of the heart.

9.10.　b, p. 291　There are four stages of regular sleep. If we count REM sleep as a separate stage of sleep, the total number of sleep stages becomes five.

9.11.　c, p. 293　Sleeping occurs primarily during REM sleep; thus, if you woke me during this stage of sleep, I could tell you what I was dreaming about.

9.12.　a, p. 295　Research on the BRAC has established that it is a 90-minute cycle of alertness under the control of the pons, and that during sleep it controls cycles of REM sleep and slow-wave sleep.

Practice Test Answers
CHAPTER 9: Practice Test 2

9.13.   d, p. 272   Modern research has not produce any evidence that suggests that animal consciousness is similar in form and content to human consciousness. Communication among members of the same animal species seems to be a reflexive, automatic process that is part of their genetic endowment.

9.14.   d, p. 274   Although people in dichotic listening tasks do not always remember hearing information that is presented to the unattended ear, that information appears to penetrate consciousness, be held in some sort of temporary memory, and exert an effect on behavior.

9.15.   a, p. 279   Whether a meditation exercises causes people to attend more closely to a stimulus or to withdraw attention from a stimulus, the function is to produce a change in one's attention and state of consciousness.

9.16.   d, p. 282   By definition, visual agnosia is the inability to recognize an object visually.

9.17.   c, p. 284   Split-brain syndrome is caused by a severing of the corpus callosum, which connects the two hemispheres. A person with split-brain syndrome is unable to communicate information that is delivered to the right hemisphere (as in the case of presenting visual stimulation to the left visual field) because that information has no way of reaching the language areas of the brain located in the left hemisphere.

9.18.   d, p. 286   By definition, hypnotic amnesia is the inability of a person who has been hypnotized to remember the events that occurred during hypnosis.

9.19.   a, p. 286   In order to determine the role of expectations about hypnosis in the subjects' behavior under hypnosis Orne (1959) led subjects to believe that one of the primary effects of hypnosis was rigidity of the preferred hand. Later he measured the rigidity of subjects' dominant hands to see what effect this information might have on subjects' behavior under hypnosis. Subjects who heard the myth showed rigidity of their dominant hands while under hypnosis; subjects who did not hear the myth did not show this symptom.

9.20.   c, p. 290   By definition, an electroencephalogram is an apparatus that records the electrical activity of the brain.

9.21.   d, p. 291   EEG recordings of the brain during stage 3 and 4 sleep do, in fact, show delta waves.

9.22.   d, p. 293   The only major effect that sleep deprivation seems to have on behavior is to interfere with performance on tasks that involve close monitoring or vigilance.

9.23.   d, p. 294   Although dreams and dreaming has been heavily researched, no one yet knows what function dreaming serves.

9.24.   d, p. 297   Cataplexy occurs during REM sleep; the other disorders listed occur during slow-wave sleep.

Practice Tests
CHAPTER 10: Practice Test 1

10.1. The branch of psychology that studies verbal behavior is called
a. phonetics.
b. psychophonology.
c. linguistics.
d. psycholinguistics.

10.2. Consider the syllable *hfis*. Although you probably have never heard this syllable before, you would likely understand its meaning if you heard in a sentence, such as "Margo caught a huge hfis below the dam today." This example reflects the importance of _____ in speech perception.
a. hearing
b. semantics
c. voicing
d. context

10.3. Content words express
a. meaning.
b. the relations between function words.
c. the surface structure of a sentence.
d. all of the above

10.4. _____ often results from damage to Broca's area.
a. Phonological dyslexia
b. Surface dyslexia
c. Isolation aphasia
d. Agrammatism

10.5. People who suffer from autotopagnosia cannot
a. write.
b. repeat words that they hear spoken.
c. produce or comprehend meaningful speech.
d. name their body parts.

10.6. In reading, the average duration of a fixation is about _____ milliseconds.
a. 100
b. 250
c. 500
d. 1000

10.7. After an injury to her brain, Celeste can not read nearly as well as she once could. Celeste appears to be suffering from a form of dyslexia known as _____ dyslexia.
a. developmental
b. acquired
c. injury-induced
d. common

10.8. If you were to read the following pairs of words in a sentence, in which pair of words would you spend the MOST amount of time fixating on the word *chair*?
    a. *arm chair*
    b. *high chair*
    c. *broken chair*
    d. *kitchen chair*

10.9. In terms of preverbal children attempting to communicate with others, which of the following does NOT belong with the other three?
    a. request
    b. rejection
    c. confirmation
    d. comment

10.10. Which of the following is NOT a characteristic of child-directed speech?
    a. an abundance of function words
    b. careful distinctions among similar sounds
    c. exaggerated intonations
    d. clear pronunciation

10.11. Nate, who is about three years old, calls his family pet, Molly, a dog. (Molly is actually a dog.) However, all other dogs he calls "kitties." This is an example of
    a. an underextension.
    b. an overextension.
    c. an inflection.
    d. both an overextension and an underextension.

10.12. Lynn said, "I goed to school." What is the most likely reply of Lynn's mother?
    a. "I went to school."
    b. "The past of the verb 'to go' is "went.'"
    c. "No, that's not right."
    d. "You must have missed language arts the day your teacher goed over verbs."

Practice Tests
CHAPTER 10: Practice Test 2

10.13. Which of the following is NOT a part of our perception of normal speech?
　　a. a series of sounds in a continuous stream
　　b. raising and lowering of pitch
　　c. a series of individual words
　　d. punctuation characterized by pauses

10.14. The _____ of a sentence tells the reader or listener who did what to whom.
　　a. word class
　　b. word order
　　c. prosody
　　d. intonation

10.15. The sentences "The girl patted her dog on his head." and "The dog was patted on his head by the girl." have _____ surface structure and _____ deep structure.
　　a. the same; a different
　　b. the same; the same
　　c. a different; a different
　　d. a different; the same

10.16. Pure word deafness is caused by
　　a. bilateral temporal lobe damage.
　　b. damage to the left parietal lobe.
　　c. an injury to both the left temporal lobe and the left parietal lobe.
　　d. damage to Broca's area.

10.17. The eye tracker is an apparatus used to
　　a. teach reading.
　　b. study eye movements.
　　c. visually follow moving objects.
　　d. scan text.

10.18. A specific deficit in reading ability that is caused by brain damage occurring after a person has already learned how to read is called _____ dyslexia.
　　a. developmental
　　b. subvocal
　　c. maturational
　　d. acquired

10.19. Abstract content words are probably BEST understood
　　a. through mental imagery.
　　b. as adjectives that modify less abstract content words.
　　c. by direct references to auditory memories.
　　d. by direct references to visual memories.

10.20. The babbling found in young children
　　a. reflects the adult speech that they hear.
　　b. contains simple words.
　　c. is their first attempt to communicate verbally.
　　d. is the same across all cultures.

10.21.	A unique string of phonemes that an infant makes is called
	a. a proneme.
	b. babbling.
	c. a protoword.
	d. cooing.

10.22.	Children tend to respond best to speech that
	a. is slightly more complex than their own.
	b. is simple.
	c. refers to tangible objects.
	d. contains no more than three words.

10.23.	Which of the following words would likely be the EASIEST for children to understand?
	a. truth
	b. larger
	c. toward
	d. rock

10.24.	One important implication of research with non-human primates in the area of symbolic communication is that
	a. true verbal ability is a social behavior.
	b. without vocal cords, non-human primates cannot communicate with humans.
	c. social interaction with humans is not necessary.
	d. all of the above

Practice Test Answers
CHAPTER 10: Practice Test 1

10.1.   d, p. 303   By definition, psycholinguistics is the branch of psychology that studies verbal behavior.

10.2.   d, p. 304   Simply hearing the syllable *hfis* gives a listener no indication of its meaning. However, if used in a sentence such as the one provided in this question, the meaning of the syllable becomes clear because of the contextual cues it provides.

10.3.   a, p. 306   By definition, a content word is a word that conveys meaning.

10.4.   d, p. 308   People who are known to have sustained damage to Broca's area often exhibit the symptoms of agrammatism.

10.5.   d, p. 312   By definition, autotopagnosia is the inability to name one's body parts.

10.6.   b, p. 314   Studies of people scanning text have revealed that the average duration of a fixation is about 250 milliseconds.

10.7.   b, p. 316   Celeste has an acquired dyslexia because she already knew how to read before she sustained brain damage. Developmental dyslexias become apparent when people are first learning how to read.

10.8.   c, p. 319   You would most likely spend more time fixating on the word *chair* if it was paired with the word *broken* because the word *broken* is not normally associated with the word *chair*. All of the other words listed are words that are commonly associated with the word *chair*.

10.9.   c, p. 322   Most attempts of preverbal children to communicate with others fall into three primary categories: rejection, request, comment. Most preverbal children do not show attempts at communication that could be classified as confirmation.

10.10.   a, p. 323   In addition to careful distinctions among similar sounds, exaggerated intonations, and clear pronunciation, child-directed speech is marked by *few* function words.

10.11.   d, p. 325   Nate's behavior is an example of an underextension because he applies the label *dog* to only one particular dog. It is also an example of an overextension because he applies the label *kitties* to all other dogs.

10.12.   a, p. 327   Most adults tend to correct children's ungrammatical speech by saying the sentence or phrase correctly

Practice Test Answers
CHAPTER 10: Practice Test 2

10.13. c, p. 303   We do not perceive speech as a string of individual words. Instead, we perceive speech to be a "stream of speech" punctuated by pauses and marked by high and low pitches.

10.14. b, p. 305   The manner in which organize words in a sentence indicates to the listener who did what do whom. For example, in the sentence, *The girl winked at her friend*, we immediately recognize it was the girl who behaved (winked) with respect to her friend.

10.15. d, p. 306   While the words in both sentences are essentially the same words, they are organized in a different order (surface structure). However, both sentences convey the same meaning (deep structure).

10.16. a, p. 310   Among the alternative answers to this question, only bilateral damage to the temporal lobes results in pure word deafness.

10.17. b, p. 314   By design, the eye tracker is intended to study the movements of the eye.

10.18. d, p. 316   By definition, an acquired dyslexia is caused by brain damage *after* a person has already learned to read.

10.19. b, p. 318   According to the text, an abstract content word such as *honesty* is often first understood in the context as an adjective that describes less abstract content words, as in *Chris is an honest person who never cheats on his taxes*.

10.20. a, p. 321   Babbling reflects both the sounds and the rhythm of the adult speech that infants hear.

10.21. c, p. 322   By definition, a protoword is a unique string of words that an infant devises and uses as a word.

10.22. a, p. 324   Children learn optimally about language when the speech they hear is just a bit more complicated than theirs. Speech that is too simple or too complicated does not adequately stimulate this learning process.

10.23. d, p. 326   Among these alternatives, the word *rock* is the only word that refers to a specific object; the other alternatives refer to relations among things. Children tend to learn relational words such as these only after they have learned simpler words such as *rock*.

10.24. a, p. 330   The most successful attempts at teaching non-human primates symbolic communication are those that involve a close working relationship between the animal and the person. In these cases, the initial attempts at communication involve nonverbal communication in social situations.

Practice Tests
CHAPTER 11: Practice Test 1

11.1. Which of the following is NOT one of the cognitive principles that are involved in Spearman's *g* factor?
   a. eduction of reasoning
   b. eduction of relations
   c. eduction of correlates
   d. apprehension of experience

11.2. The extent to which a person possesses crystallized intelligence depends on his or her
   a. experiences.
   b. level of fluid intelligence.
   c. intellectual environment.
   d. all of the above

11.3. People who sustain damage to their _____ are still able to perform quite well on standard intelligence tests, which provides partial support for _____ theory of intelligence.
   a. frontal lobes; Sternberg's
   b. amygdala; Cattell's
   c. occipital lobe; Thurstone's
   d. association cortex; Gardner's

11.4. Modern intelligence tests originated in _____ with the work of _____.
   a. England; Galton
   b. France; Binet
   c. the United States; Terman
   d. Germany; Wechsler

11.5. _____ revised the Binet-Simon scale for use in the United States.
   a. Stanford
   b. Wechsler
   c. Sternberg
   d. Terman

11.6. Jan took an IQ test two years ago and scored 126. She took the same IQ test a week ago and scored 128. Apparently, this IQ test has a high degree of
   a. validity.
   b. accuracy.
   c. reliability.
   d. generality.

11.7. Which of the following statements is TRUE?
   a. The heritability of a given trait depends on the amount of genetic variability present in a given person at a given time.
   b. The relative importance of environmental factors in a trait depends on the amount of environmental variability present in the population.
   c. The heritability of any given trait is modulated by the extent to which genetic and environmental factors exert independent influences on that trait at any given time in any given population.
   d. all of the above

62

11.8. The lowest correlation in intelligence is likely to occur between
    a. a brother and sister raised together.
    b. a biological parent and child living together.
    c. a biological parent and child living apart.
    d. two sisters raised apart.

11.9. Classifying people on the basis of race alone is difficult and probably inconclusive in terms of intelligence, based on the fact that
    a. people of different races interbreed.
    b. skin pigmentation is uncorrelated with many psychological and physical traits.
    c. so many environmental factors affect people's physical and intellectual abilities.
    d. all of the above

11.10. Concepts
    a. are inferences made from the rules of language.
    b. are logical constructions made from legitimate premises.
    c. represent the important characteristics of a category.
    d. exist because the characteristics of objects and situations have consequences for us.

11.11. The argument that people do not look up the meanings of concepts in their heads in the same way that they look up meanings of words in a dictionary was made by
    a. Rosch.
    b. Collins and Quillian.
    c. Smith.
    d. Johnson-Laird.

11.12. A mental construction based on physical reality that is used to solve problems involving deductive reasoning is called a(n)
    a. exemplar.
    b. mental model.
    c. metaphor.
    d. natural concept.

Practice Tests
CHAPTER 11: Practice Test 2

11.13. Thurstone argued that intelligence involved _____ factors.
   a. 1
   b. 2
   c. 7
   d. 10

11.14. When she first encountered a particular type of calculus problem, Holli had difficulty solving it. Now that she has practiced this sort of problem, she is able to solve it quite easily, including those problems that are novel to her. Apparently, at least for solving this sort of calculus problem, Holli is high in _____ intelligence.
   a. contextual
   b. componential
   c. experiential
   d. adaptive

11.15. The kind of intelligence observed among traditional tribal peoples is
   a. inferior to that of Western cultures.
   b. absent of logical reasoning.
   c. essentially the same as the intelligence observed among people living in Western cultures.
   d. based on the application of logic to facts gained through direct experience.

11.16. To assess a child's intellectual ability, Binet and Simon (1905),
   a. administered several sensory discrimination tests to children of various ages.
   b. devised an overall point rating system ranging from below average to above average.
   c. formulated the IQ quotient.
   d. compared the child's performance relative to an established age-determined average.

11.17. A deviation IQ score of 164 falls how many standard deviations above the mean for this kind of IQ score?
   a. 0
   b. 1
   c. 2
   d. 3

11.18. Jarmane is mentally retarded. However, he is able to live on his own and has a job in his community. Jarmane would most likely be classified as being _____ retarded.
   a. mildly
   b. profoundly
   c. borderline
   d. slightly

11.19. Mental retardation is caused by
   a. certain environmental factors.
   b. genetic factors.
   c. factors that affect normal brain development.
   d. all of the above

11.20. In terms of both biological and adoptive families, which of the following intellectual abilities is the least correlated in terms of the parent-child relationship?
   a. math
   b. vocabulary
   c. block design
   d. picture arrangement

11.21. Thinking involves
   a. categorizing.
   b. reasoning.
   c. problem solving.
   d. all of the above

11.22. If you had been a subject in Collins and Quillian's study, to which of the statements below would your response time have been MOST likely to be the FASTEST?
   a. "A salmon is a fish."
   b. "A salmon swims upstream to lay eggs."
   c. "A salmon has gills."
   d. "A salmon can move around."

11.23. An argument composed of two or more premises from which a conclusion is intended to follow logically is an example of
   a. inductive reasoning.
   b. deductive reasoning.
   c. a heuristic.
   d. an algorithm.

11.24. _____ consists of inferring general principles from specific facts.
   a. Deductive reasoning
   b. Creating a mental model
   c. Creative thinking
   d. Inductive reasoning

Practice Test Answers
CHAPTER 11: Practice Test 1

11.1.   a, p. 336   The three cognitive principles involved in Spearman's *g* factor are eduction of reasoning, eduction of correlates, and apprehension of experience.

11.2.   d, p. 337   The level of crystallized intelligence that one possesses depends heavily on one's learning experiences (which depends heavily on one's personal experiences), one's intellectual environment, and one's level of fluid intelligence.

11.3.   a, p. 340   It is true that people who sustain damage to their frontal lobes can still perform well on standardized tests of intelligence. However, they perform poorly in other areas, such as planning activities in their daily lives. Sternberg's theory asserts that intelligence is more than a score on an IQ test; it also has something to do with carrying out day to day activities efficiently. Thus, in Sternberg's view, this sort of brain damage does in fact affect one's intelligence.

11.4.   b, p. 343   Alfred Binet developed the first intelligence test for use in the French school system.

11.5.   d, p. 344   Lewis Terman adapted the Binet-Simon test for use in the United States.

11.6.   c, p. 346   A reliable IQ test is one in which a person who takes it twice will achieve similar scores each time.

11.7.   b, p. 349   If environmental variability is low, then the role of the environment is minimal. However if environmental variability is high, then the role of the environment is responsible for much of the variability in intelligence. All other alternatives to this question are false.

11.8.   d, p. 352   Table 11.6 on page 352 indicates that among the genetic relationships listed, the lowest correlation in intelligence is found between two siblings who are raised apart.

11.9.   d, p. 354   Classifying people according to race is tricky stuff for several reasons. First, people of different races interbreed, making assignment of offspring to a particular race difficult. Second, skin color is not very highly correlated with any psychological attributes. And third, environmental factors figure prominently in both physical and intellectual matters.

11.10. d, p. 357   We tend to define concepts and place them into categories based on their significance to us. Depending on how things affect us personally, we may place them into different categories relative to others for whom those things have different personal relevance.

11.11. a, p. 358   It was Rosch who made this argument; she also stated that people's natural concepts involved collections of exemplars.

11.12. b, p. 360   By definition, a mental model is a mental construction of reality based on physical reality that is used to solve problems involving deduction.

Practice Test Answers
CHAPTER 11: Practice Test 2

11.13.   c, p. 337   Based on his work with college students, Lewis Thurstone argued that intelligence involves seven distinct factors.

11.14.   c, p. 339   By definition, experiential intelligence involves the ability to solve previously encountered problems automatically. In this case, this is exactly what Holli is able to do.

11.15.   d, p. 342   Cross-cultural research has shown that traditional tribal peoples are readily able to apply logical reasoning to factual information that has been acquired through experience.

11.16.   d, p. 344   Binet and Simon compared children's scores on an IQ test with established norms for children of different ages.

11.17.   d, p. 345   As can be seen in Figure 11.3 on page 345, an IQ score of 164 falls three standard deviations above the mean for scores on this IQ test.

11.18.   a, p. 348   People who are moderately retarded are able to lead independent lives and perform well at most tasks that are not intellectually challenging.

11.19.   d, p. 350   Researchers have clearly established that mental retardation can be caused by a variety of factors including genetic variables, environmental variables, and brain damage.

11.20.   d, p. 353   As Table 11.7 on page 353 indicates, picture arrangement has the lowest correlation among parent-child relationships in both biological and adoptive families.

11.21.   d, p. 356   By definition, thinking involves categorizing, reasoning, and problem solving.

11.22.   b, p. 357   The results of the Collins and Quillian study showed that their subjects responded fastest to characteristics that were specific to a particular concept. Of the alternative answers given in this question, the only characteristic that is specific to salmon is that they swim upstream to lay eggs.

11.23.   b, p. 359   Deductive reasoning involves inferring specific instances from general principles or rules. A syllogism, which is composed of two or more premises from which a specific conclusion follows, is an example of an exercise in deductive reasoning.

11.24.   d, p. 362   By definition, inductive reasoning involves the inferring of general principles from specific facts.

Practice Tests
CHAPTER 12: Practice Test 1

12.1.	The internal organs of the fetus begin to form during the _____ stage of prenatal development.
a. ovulatory
b. zygote
c. embryo
d. fetal

12.2.	According to Piaget, _____ are mental representations that describe events and their relation to other concepts.
a. concepts
b. schemata
c. cognitions
d. hypotheses

12.3.	If an object is completely hidden from view after a 12-16-month-old infant has observed it, the infant will
a. lose interest in the object.
b. continue to stare at the spot at which the object disappeared.
c. begin crying and screaming.
d. search for the object in the last place that he or she saw it hidden.

12.4.	Which of the following appears to be a valid criticism of the effects of television viewing on the cognitive development of children?
a. Television viewing mesmerizes children.
b. Television viewing could probably do more to foster cognitive development.
c. Television viewing overstimulates children.
d. Television viewing impairs cognitive development in most children.

12.5.	In the Strange Situation, an infant who shows moderate signs of distress when her mother leaves, but who is easily consoled upon her return is considered to be _____ attached.
a. securely
b. resistantly
c. avoidantly
d. ambivalently

12.6.	Among young monkeys, social interaction is important for learning
a. how to deal with fear.
b. when to assume dominant behaviors.
c. when not to challenge a more aggressive monkey.
d. all of the above

12.7.	By the age of _____ children begin to perceive themselves as boys or as girls.
a. 18 months
b. 2 years
c. 30 months
d. 3 years

12.8. A prominent difference in the way parents socialize their sons and daughters involves
   a. a difference in the amount of time they spend playing with a son or a daughter.
   b. a difference in the amount of time they spend just talking with a son or a daughter.
   c. a difference in the kinds of clothes they select for a son or daughter to wear.
   d. differences in the kinds of encouragement they offer for "gender-appropriate" play.

12.9. A criticism of Kohlberg's theory of moral development is that it is _____. Research has shown this criticism to be _____.
   a. vague and ambiguous; valid
   b. vague and ambiguous; invalid
   c. gender-biased; accurate
   d. gender-biased; inaccurate

12.10. Rudman found that injections of _____ had the effect of increasing _____ in elderly men.
   a. estrogen; masses of the liver and spleen
   b. human growth hormone; muscle mass
   c. testosterone; body fat
   d. dopamine; skin thickness

12.11. Intelligence that reflects both knowledge and experience is called _____ intelligence.
   a. expert
   b. pragmatic
   c. fluid
   d. crystallized

12.12. Of the five stages in Kübler-Ross's conception of death and dying only _____ is considered to be universal.
   a. anger
   b. denial
   c. acceptance
   d. depression

Practice Tests
CHAPTER 12: Practice Test 2

12.13. One of the negative side effects of a woman smoking during her pregnancy is that the fetus may be
   a. born with a cleft palate.
   b. born severely mentally retarded.
   c. born with a limited respiration capacity.
   d. aborted or born prematurely.

12.14. The period in which a child first grasps the concept of object permanence is the _____ period.
   a. sensorimotor
   b. preoperational
   c. concrete operational
   d. formal operational

12.15. The end of the _____ period of cognitive development coincides with the beginning of adolescence.
   a. sensorimotor
   b. preoperational
   c. concrete operational
   d. formal operational

12.16. Mothers of securely attached babies tend to
   a. be adept at holding and caressing their babies.
   b. attend to their babies more inconsistently.
   c. encourage less physical contact.
   d. have unrealistic ideas about parenting.

12.17. Mothers who seem insensitive to their baby's needs are likely to foster _____ attachment.
   a. secure
   b. resistant
   c. avoidant
   d. ambivalent

12.18. Many of the potential negative aspects of parental divorce on a child's natural growth and development are lessened when
   a. there is little or no conflict between the child's parents.
   b. the child has plenty of interaction with both parents.
   c. after the divorce, the parents cooperate pleasantly with each other in raising the child.
   d. all of the above

12.19. Which of the following has been shown to be a reliable gender difference?
   a. Boys show earlier verbal development.
   b. Girls show stronger spatial abilities.
   c. Girls are more likely to show early language disorders.
   d. Girls show a higher tendency toward compliance.

12.20. Kohlberg's method for studying the development of moral reasoning was to
   a. ask children to respond to stories involving moral dilemmas.
   b. conduct cross-sectional research.
   c. conduct a series of cross-cultural studies involving moral dilemmas.
   d. place children in positions in which their honesty and truthfulness could be tested and observed.

12.21. The first visible sign of the development of adult secondary sexual characteristics in females is
   a. the growth of pubic hair.
   b. a spurt in growth.
   c. menstruation.
   d. accumulation of fatty tissue in the breasts.

12.22. Schaie's research has shown that many of our intellectual abilities increase until the _____ and then remain stable until _____.
   a. mid 20s; early 30s
   b. late 20s; late 30s or early 40s
   c. late 40s; mid 50s or early 60s
   d. late 30s or early 40s; mid 50s or early 60s.

12.23. The fact that older people tend to perform intellectual tasks more slowly than younger people is attributable to
   a. deterioration of sensory functioning.
   b. the tendency of older people to be cautious in their behavior.
   c. difficulty in changing strategies to meet new demands.
   d. all of the above

12.24. Although Kübler-Ross's work has been criticized, it is not without its merits. One merit is that it has
   a. raised scientific and public awareness of the plight of the terminally ill.
   b. prompted more research into death and dying.
   c. stimulated public support for the terminally ill and their families.
   d. all of the above

Practice Test Answers
CHAPTER 12: Practice Test 1

12.1. b, p. 371 Studies of fetal development have shown that the internal organs begin to develop during the zygote stage of prenatal development.

12.2. b, p. 378 According to Piaget, schemata are cognitive structures that consist of mental representations that describe events and their relation to other concepts.

12.3. d, p. 379 By the time an infant is 12 to 16 months old, object permanence has developed; this means that once an object has been observed and later hidden, the infant will initiate a search for it beginning in the place where it was last seen.

12.4. b, p. 386 Among the alternative answers listed in this question, the only criticism that is backed up by actual research support is the notion that television could provide more intellectual stimulation for children.

12.5. a, p. 390 By definition, a securely attached infant is an infant who will show moderate signs of distress at her mother's departure but is easily consoled on her return.

12.6. d, p. 392 Early social experiences in monkeys provide learning experiences for future social interactions as an adult. In particular it is during these early social experiences that monkeys learn about fear and the dominance structure of their troops.

12.7. b, p. 394 The self-perception that one is a boy or a girl occurs at about the age of two years. At age eighteen months, children are not cognitively capable of such a perception. By age thirty months, a child has already acquired such a self-perception.

12.8. d, p. 396 Although parents socialize their sons and daughters in many different ways, the most profound difference in this process is the encouragement of "gender-appropriate" play.

12.9. d, p. 398 Gilligan suggested that Kohlberg's theory of moral development is gender-biased. However, research has not supported Gilligan's contention.

12.10. b, p. 404 Rudman's research did, in fact, establish that injections of human growth hormone into elderly men produced increases in muscle mass.

12.11. d, p. 407 By definition, crystallized intelligence is intelligence that reflects both knowledge and experience.

12.12. b, p. 409 The extensive research conducted on Kübler-Ross's proposed five stages of dealing with the knowledge that one is dying has only supported the existence of the denial stage.

Practice Test Answers
CHAPTER 12: Practice Test 2

12.13. d, p. 372   Many analyses of the effects of a mother's cigarette smoking on her fetus have established that cigarette smoking may cause the baby either to be aborted or to be born prematurely.

12.14. a, p. 379   Studies of the cognitive development of children have established that it is during the first of Piaget's periods, the sensorimotor period, that infants initially acquire object permanence.

12.15. c, p. 382   The last period of Piaget's conception of cognitive development in children, the period of concrete operations, marks the transition from childhood to adolescence.

12.16. a, p. 391   One of the important characteristics of mothers who have securely attached babies is that they tend to be skilled at holding and caressing their infants.

12.17. c, p. 391   Studies of attachment have established that avoidantly attached infants have mothers who tend to seem insensitive to the infant's needs.

12.18. d, p. 393   The key factor influencing the effects of divorce on a child's social development is the extent to which his or her parents cooperate and get along with each other. Children of divorced parents who fight a lot show deficits in social development; children of divorced parents who get along well show fewer signs of defective social development.

12.19. d, p. 394   Of the alternatives listed in this question, the only gender difference that research has established to be reliable is the tendency of girls to be more compliant than boys.

12.20. a, p. 397   The basic feature of Kohlberg's research on moral development were the stories involving particular moral dilemmas that children read and then were "quizzed" on later.

12.21. d, p. 400   The first noticeable secondary sexual characteristic of female sexual development is the accumulation of fatty tissue in the breasts.

12.22. d, p. 405   Schaie's longitudinal studies of adult intellectual development has shown that our intellectual abilities increase into our late 30s or early 40s and remain stable into our mid 50s or early 60s.

12.23. d, p. 407   As people get older, they tend to be less flexible and more cautious in their thinking, and they show some signs that their sensory systems don't work as well as they used to. Combined, these factors would appear to explain why older people often perform more poorly than younger people on intellectual tasks.

12.24. d, p. 409   Although her conception of the stages of dealing with the certainty that one is dying seems to be inaccurate, Kübler-Ross's theory of death and dying has heightened both public and scientific awareness of the plight of the terminally ill. In turn, this awareness has stimulated public support for the terminally ill and their families and has led to more scientific research on death and dying.

Practice Tests
CHAPTER 13: Practice Test 1

13.1. An unpleasant internal state caused by a homeostatic unbalance that motivates behavior is called a
a. negative feedback loop.
b. drive.
c. set point.
d. detector variable.

13.2. The extent to which people may persist in emitting a particular behavior may be influenced by
a. intermittent reinforcement.
b. conditioned reinforcement.
c. the satisfaction they receive from emitting that behavior.
d. all of the above

13.3. An early theory of hunger proposed by Cannon asserted that people are motivated to eat when their
a. hypothalamuses signal the nervous system that blood-sugar levels are low.
b. temporary fat reservoirs are low.
c. set points for food are triggered by signals from the brain.
d. stomachs are empty.

13.4. Ann drank two glasses of milk and Carol drank two glasses of water before supper. Most likely
a. Ann will eat more food for supper than Carol.
b. Carol will eat more food for supper than Ann.
c. both women will eat about the same amount of food for supper.
d. neither woman will be hungry at supper.

13.5. Jody is a 21-year-old college student who is obsessed with her body weight. She feels that she is too heavy, even though she weighs only 100 pounds (she is 5'1" tall). She will sometimes go for several days without eating food but will drink large amounts of diet soda. Occasionally she will go on an eating rampage, consuming large quantities of food, only to relieve herself using laxatives. What would you diagnose Jody's eating problem to be?
a. obesity
b. anorexia nervosa
c. bulimia
d. both anorexia and bulimia

13.6. Women who take oral contraceptives
a. enjoy sexual intercourse more than women who use other forms of birth control.
b. show little fluctuation in sexual interest across the menstrual cycle.
c. show peaks of sexual activity during the third week of the menstrual cycle.
d. show decreased sexual desire compared to women who use other forms of birth control.

13.7. Females who experienced prenatal exposure to high levels of androgens
a. have a reduced desire for sexual activity in adulthood.
b. may develop a higher than average tendency to toward homosexuality.
c. develop male external genitalia.
d. report engaging in more sexual activity as adults than females who experienced prenatal exposure to normal levels of androgens.

13.8. Research on the effects of viewing violence on television may be summarized by stating that
a. the link between long-term viewing of television violence and later aggression is firmly established.
b. a link between long-term viewing of television violence and later aggression has not been established.
c. a link between long-term viewing of television violence may cause an increase in later aggressive behavior among girls but not among boys.
d. a link between long-term viewing of television violence may cause an increase in later aggressive behavior.

13.9. The orbitofrontal cortex has neural connections to the
a. basal ganglia.
b. amygdala.
c. cerebellum.
d. all of the above

13.10. A potential problem with the use of the guilty knowledge test in lie detection is
a. false positives.
b. that it is easy to accuse an innocent person of committing an illegal act.
c. the extent to which the polygraphers know the details of an event.
d. all of the above

13.11. Young blind children
a. do not show facial expressions of emotion.
b. tend to overexpress emotion in terms of their facial expressions.
c. tend to use their hands and body language to convey emotion to others.
d. show facial expressions of emotion that are very similar to those of sighted children.

13.12. According to James, we
a. feel sorry because we cry.
b. cry because we feel sorry.
c. feel sorry and cry because of socialization processes.
d. feel sorry and cry because of innate brain mechanisms.

Practice Tests
CHAPTER 13: Practice Test 2

13.13. That you seek an alternative activity when you are bored by a present one and seek rest when you are tired would be best predicted by psychologists who subscribe to _____ theory.
   a. drive reduction
   b. need
   c. incentive
   d. optimum-level

13.14. According to Seligman, learned helplessness has
   a. no experimental support.
   b. the characteristics of a personality trait.
   c. its roots in optimum arousal theory.
   d. applications for understanding schizophrenic disorders.

13.15. Fatty acids are to the _____ as glucose is to the _____.
   a. hypothalamus; pancreas
   b. body; brain
   c. Cannon and Washburn theory; glucostatic hypothesis
   d. short-term reservoir; long-term reservoir

13.16. Psychological depression seems to
   a. be an important cause of obesity.
   b. be an important effect of becoming obese.
   c. totally unrelated to obesity.
   d. be partially caused by the secretion of leptin.

13.17. If a male is castrated, his ability to achieve an erection and to ejaculate
   a. are diminished immediately.
   b. cannot be restored through supplements of testosterone.
   c. are still retained for many years.
   d. may be lost immediately or gradually, depending on individual differences.

13.18. Tim is happy and outgoing. Les is shy and insecure. Kermit is unhappy and has some emotional problems. Which of these persons is most likely to be homosexual?
   a. Tim
   b. Les
   c. Kermit
   d. none of the above

13.19. Mark the mouse was raised in a cage all by himself. When he was about 6 months old, Mickey the mouse was placed into Mark's cage. However, Mark did not attack Mickey. Mark's lack of aggression suggests that
   a. Mickey was castrated early in life.
   b. Mickey immediately made an appeasement gesture.
   c. Mark immediately made an appeasement gesture.
   d. Mark was castrated early in life.

13.20. A coping response
   a. seems likely to involve negative reinforcement.
   b. can be learned.
   c. may involve the termination of an aversive stimulus.
   d. all of the above

13.21. One effect of the prefrontal lobotomy is
   a. the inability to carry out plans.
   b. increased sexual arousal.
   c. the inability to restrain oneself from becoming aggressive.
   d. none of the above

13.22. Darwin argued that emotional expressions in people and in non-human animals are
   a. learned.
   b. innate.
   c. composed of simple movements of face, neck, and head.
   d. primarily reactions to aversive environmental events.

13.23. One of Ekman's studies revealed that when alone, Japanese and American students _____, but when they were in the presence of another the _____ students expressed _____ than the _____ students.
   a. showed about the same amount of emotion; American; less; Japanese
   b. showed about the same amount of emotion; Japanese; less; American
   c. showed no emotion; Japanese; more; American
   d. showed no emotion; American; more; Japanese

13.24. The idea that emotions are produced only by cognitive processes has been argued by
   a. Ekman.
   b. Lazarus.
   c. Lange.
   d. Zajonc.

Practice Test Answers
CHAPTER 13: Practice Test 1

13.1. b, p. 416   By definition, a drive is an unpleasant state caused by a homeostatic disequilibrium that motivates behavior.

13.2. d, p. 418   People's behavior is influenced by many variables; chief among those variables are experience with reinforcement (both intermittent and conditioned reinforcement) and the enjoyment or satisfaction provided by engaging in those behaviors.

13.3. d, p. 421   Walter Cannon did, in fact, propose that hunger is caused simply by the stomach being empty.

13.4. b, p. 422   The food detectors in Amy's stomach will detect the chemicals present in the milk she drank. These detectors will signal the brain that food is present in the stomach and eating will be regulated accordingly. The detectors in Carol's stomach will detect the presence of water but will not signal the brain that food is present because water does not contain the same kinds of chemical that milk does. Therefore, Carol is likely to eat more food at supper than Amy.

13.5. d, p. 424   Jody is showing behaviors typical of both anorexia and bulimia.

13.6. b, p. 427   Alexander's et al.'s (1990) research showed that consumption of oral contraception had little or no effects on changing a woman's sexual interest during her menstrual cycle.

13.7. b, p. 429   Money et al.'s (1984) research that women who were exposed to androgens prenatally were several times more likely than women who were exposed to normal levels of prenatal androgens to exhibit homosexual tendencies.

13.8. d, p. 432   Field studies involving boys' long-term viewing of watching television violence suggests that this pattern of viewing is moderately correlated with the boys' tendencies to be aggressive later in life.

13.9. b, p. 434   Basic anatomical studies of the brain show that the orbitofrontal cortex has neuronal connections to the amygdala.

13.10. c, p. 437   If polygraphers are unaware of certain details of the commission of a crime, they cannot develop relevant questions to ask the suspect.

13.11. d, p. 440   Although young blind children have never observed another person's facial expression, they nevertheless show facial expressions that resemble those of other people.

13.12. a, p. 442   According to James, we feel an emotion based on our interpretation of our physiological responses to environmental events. Thus, he would argue that "we feel sorry because we cry."

Practice Test Answers
CHAPTER 13: Practice Test 2

13.13.   d, p. 417   The optimal level hypothesis states that we will engage in behavior that returns our level of arousal to an optimal level. Thus, if we are tired we might rest and if we are bored we might seek stimulation.

13.14.   b, p. 419   Seligman's research and thinking on learned helplessness has led him to suggest that learned helplessness becomes a more or less permanent pattern of behavior in people who have extensive histories of failure.

13.15.   b, p. 421   The primary energy source for the brain is glucose and the primary energy source for the body is fatty acids.

13.16.   b, p. 423   According to research on obesity conducted by Rodin and her colleagues, depression is more likely to be a result than a cause of obesity.

13.17.   d, p. 426   Men who are castrated experience decreases in their sex drive accompanied by failure to achieve erections and to ejaculate. However, possibly due to differences in their sexual experiences prior to castration, some men show deficits in sexual performance earlier than other men.

13.18.   d, p. 428   Many research studies indicate that a person's level of psychological adjustment cannot be predicted on the basis of his or her sexual orientation.

13.19.   d, p. 430   Mice that are castrated early in life, like Mark the mouse was, show unusually low levels of aggression when another mouse is placed in their cage. Normal mice will show very aggressive behavior toward the intruder.

13.20.   d, p. 433   A coping response is any response that terminates, avoids, or minimizes an aversive stimulus. Thus, people appear to learn how to cope in those situations that involve negative reinforcement.

13.21.   a, p. 435   Patients who have undergone a prefrontal lobotomy show profound deficits in their ability to carry out plans.

13.22.   b, p. 438   Darwin believed that emotions in all animals are the products of biological evolution. He further believed that the expression of these emotions are not learned behavior patterns, but rather are inherited.

13.23.   b, p. 441   Ekman's research on cross-cultural differences in emotional expression showed that American and Japanese people express emotion similarly when alone but differently when in the presence of others. These differences presumably occur because American and Japanese people are socialized differently with respect to interacting with others.

13.24.   b, p. 443   Lazarus (1984) has long argued that cognition is a necessary component of emotion. In fact, Ekman has suggested that emotions are only produced through the anticipation, the experiencing, or the imaging of outcomes produced by interacting with the environment.

Practice Tests
CHAPTER 14: Practice Test 1

14.1. _____ argued that there are _____ personality traits.
    a. Allport; 5
    b. Eysenck; 16
    c. Cattell; 16
    d. McCrae; 3

14.2. In Eysenck's model of personality, _____ is considered to be the polar opposite of psychoticism.
    a. self-control
    b. emotional stability
    c. neuroticism
    d. apprehension

14.3. Which of the following aspects of personality do NOT appear to be influenced by heredity?
    a. belief in God
    b. attitudes toward racial integration
    c. masculinity/femininity
    d. all of the above

14.4. An important figure in the history of the social learning approach who blended his ideas on cognition with Skinner's ideas on behavior is
    a. Bandura.
    b. Adler.
    c. Zuckerman.
    d. Maslow.

14.5. Jamaal has made three attempts to pass the road test for his driver's license. He now is beginning to think that no matter what he does or how much he practices, he will never get his license. Jamaal's view of his present situation would seem to fit Rotter's idea of
    a. self-efficacy.
    b. reciprocal determinism.
    c. internal locus of control.
    d. external locus of control.

14.6. Which of the following statements is TRUE?
    a. Situational variables are stronger than personality traits in predicting behavior.
    b. Personality traits are stronger than situational variables in predicting behavior.
    c. Powerful situations have no impact on behavior; rather, they impact cognition.
    d. Personality traits and situational variables interact to determine behavior.

14.7. The primary source of instinctual motivation is _____, which is stored in the _____.
    a. psychic energy; ego
    b. the ego; unconscious
    c. libido; id
    d. libido; superego

14.8. A person who behaves in a manner directly opposite of how he or she really feels is using a defense mechanism called
    a. reaction formation.
    b. compensation.
    c. sublimation.
    d. rationalization.

14.9. According to Freud, the central issue in the Oedipus complex is that the young boy unconsciously
    a. lusts after his mother, but can never really have her sexually.
    b. desires to kill his mother.
    c. begins to seek normal adult sexual gratification.
    d. wishes he could have a baby.

14.10. Freud and Erikson agreed that
    a. sexuality plays an important role in the development of personality.
    b. libido is a destructive force in personality development.
    c. anxiety is a widespread problem that interferes with normal personality development.
    d. stages of development are marked by crises and how these crises are resolved affects personality development.

14.11. The criticisms of the humanistic approach include its
    a. reliance on subjective concepts.
    b. tendency to describe rather than explain personality.
    c. failure to generate research.
    d. all of the above

14.12. The number of questions that a person fails to answer on the MMPI is reflected in the _____ scale.
    a. ?
    b. L
    c. K
    d. F

Practice Tests
CHAPTER 14: Practice Test 2

14.13.   Cattell's research on personality was based on the earlier work of
   a. Galen.
   b. Eysenck.
   c. Mischel.
   d. Allport.

14.14.   Which two traits of the five-factor model appear to have the strongest research support regarding their biological basis?
   a. openness and agreeableness
   b. conscientiousness and psychoticism
   c. neuroticism and extraversion
   d. introversion and openness

14.15.   Byron is a shy 2-year-old. According to research on shyness, Byron will
   a. eventually outgrow his shyness.
   b. become less shy depending on his social experiences during adolescence.
   c. have about a 50 percent change of remaining shy as an adult.
   d. grow up to be a shy child.

14.16.   Marcus is considering trying out for the third base position on his college's baseball team. After watching the team's regular third baseman at practice, he changes his mind. In the language of social learning theory, Marcus's decision was based on his
   a. ability to learn vicariously.
   b. ability to modify his behavior and thinking through observational learning.
   c. locus of control.
   d. self-efficacy.

14.17.   The people who have been found to have the highest levels of internal locus of control, based on scores from the I-E scale, were
   a. Peace Corps volunteers.
   b. environmentalists.
   c. CEOs of Fortune 500 companies.
   d. professional athletes.

14.18.   Before Freud's work became well known, many people believed that behavior was determined by
   a. unconscious forces.
   b. spirits and demons.
   c. conscious rational forces.
   d. the interaction of biological and environmental variables.

14.19.   According to Freud, "_____ is the royal road to a knowledge of the unconscious activities of the mind."
   a. Free association
   b. Transference
   c. The interpretation of dreams
   d. Understanding childhood experiences

14.20. An unconscious obsession with an erogenous zone due to failure to resolve a crisis during the corresponding stage of psychosexual development is called
a. anxiety.
b. regression.
c. repression.
d. fixation.

14.21. Universal thought forms and patterns that represent the common experiences that we share with our ancestors were termed _____ by Jung.
a. attitudes
b. basic orientations
c. collective forms
d. archetypes

14.22. Which of the following is NOT a characteristic of the historical figures that Maslow consider to be self-actualized?
a. self-accepting
b. open to others' opinions and ideas
c. spontaneous in their emotional reactions
d. had many friends

14.23. The current version of the MMPI is called the
a. MMPI-R
b. Revised MMPI
c. MMPI-2
d. none of the above

14.24. Becky, who often has difficulty expressing herself and will not admit that she has any personal problems, is about to take the MMPI-2. Which of the validity scales will reflect these aspects of Becky's personality?
a. L
b. F
c. ?
d. K

Practice Test Answers
CHAPTER 14: Practice Test 1

14.1.   c, p. 451   Cattell has argued that personality consists of 16 factors; Eysenck has argued for 3 factors; McCrae has argued for 5; and Allport did not argue for any specific number of traits.

14.2.   a, p. 452   By definition, self-control is at the opposite end of the continuum from psychoticism.

14.3.   d, p. 456   Heredity does not influence acquired beliefs and behaviors such as belief in God, attitudes toward race issues, or exhibiting masculine or feminine behaviors.

14.4.   a, p. 458   Bandura is considered to be the founder of social learning theory, which blends Skinner's notion of reinforcement with Bandura's conception of how cognitive processes influence behavior.

14.5.   d, p. 460   People like Jamaal, who perceive that they have no control over the events that occur in their lives, are said to possess an external locus of control.

14.6.   d, p. 462   After heated debate, many psychologists now believe that neither personality traits nor a person's personal situation, alone, determine behavior. Instead, behavior is believed to be the product of the interaction of these variables.

14.7.   c, p. 464   According to Freud, the libido, which is housed in the id, is the primary source of psychic energy.

14.8.   a, p. 466   By definition, a reaction formation is a defense mechanism that involves behaving in a manner directly opposite of the way that one truly feels (because these true feelings produce anxiety).

14.9.   a, p. 468   By definition, the Oedipus complex centers on the boy's unconscious sexual desire for his mother. However, in reality, the boy can never achieve this desire because of the presence of his father.

14.10.   d, p. 470   Both Freud and Erikson proposed stage theories of development. However, Freud's theory centered on sexuality and Erikson's theory on psychosocial development.

14.11.   d, p. 474   Humanistic theory has generated little valuable research in the area of personality because its concepts are subjective and it is more descriptive than it is explanatory.

14.12.   a, p. 475   By design, the ? scale of the MMPI includes a tally of the number of questions the person does not answer.

Practice Test Answers
CHAPTER 14: Practice Test 2

14.13. d, p. 451 Allport was the first person to search systematically for the basic traits of personality. His work stimulated others, including Cattell, to search for the basic traits of which personality is composed.

14.14. c, p. 454 Based on the existing research on the heritability of personality traits, neuroticism and extraversion have been found to be most closely linked to a genetic basis for personality.

14.15. d, p. 457 Kagan and his colleagues (1988) found shyness to be an enduring trait; people who are shy as children tend to be shy as adults.

14.16. d, p. 459 Self-efficacy is one's expectations for success in a particular situation. In this case, Marcus decided that he was not as good as the team's regular third basemen and so he decided not to try out for the team with respect to that position.

14.17. a, p. 460 Rotter's (1966) research using the I-E Scale has shown that people with the highest level of internal loci of control are indeed people who served as volunteers in the Peace Corps.

14.18. c, p. 463 Freud was the first person to argue effectively that much human behavior is due to unconscious forces.

14.19. c, p. 465 This question involves a direct quote from Freud on the topic of the interpretation of dreams.

14.20. d, p. 467 By definition, a fixation is an unconscious obsession with an erogenous zone (caused by failure to resolve the relevant crisis) during a stage of psychosexual development.

14.21. d, p. 469 By Jung's definition, an archetype is a universal thought form or pattern that represents the common experiences in life that we share with our ancestors.

14.22. d, p. 472 According to Maslow, people who are self-actualized tend to be self-accepting, open to others' ideas and opinions, spontaneous in the expression of their emotions, and have a few very close friends (rather than many superficial ones).

14 23. c, p. 475 The MMPI-2 is the name of the current version of the MMPI.

14.24. d, p. 476 By design, the K scale of the MMPI is intended to identify people who try to hide their true feelings while taking the test. This scale is likely to identify Becky as a person who has this tendency.

Practice Tests
CHAPTER 15: Practice Test 1

15.1. A person's unique individuality is called
   a. a self-concept.
   b. the self.
   c. self-esteem.
   d. personality.

15.2. Attribution involves people focusing on two different types of causes:
   a. cognitive and behavioral.
   b. dispositional and situational.
   c. biological and environmental.
   d. social and nonsocial.

15.3. The tendency of people to explain their behavior in terms of situational factors and others' behavior in terms of dispositional factors is termed
   a. belief in a just world.
   b. the actor-observer effect.
   c. the distinctiveness principle.
   d. self-serving bias.

15.4. When Jarrad sees Maggie, Maggie always smiles and is extremely nice. Now every time Jarrad sees her, he feels happy and excited. Jarrad's attitude toward Maggie was influenced by
   a. modeling.
   b. direct classical conditioning.
   c. vicarious classical conditioning.
   d. none of the above

15.5. If we find ourselves avoiding people who pierce their noses and lips, we are likely to conclude that we have a negative attitude toward people who are "into" such forms of body piercing. This is an example of which factor that influences attitude-behavior relations?
   a. the degree of specificity of the attitude
   b. self-attribution
   c. the motivational relevance of behavior
   d. constraints on behavior

15.6. The theory that we come to understand our attitudes and emotions by observing our own behavior and the circumstances under which it occurs is called _____ theory.
   a. self-attribution
   b. cognitive dissonance
   c. self-perception
   d. self-schema

15.7. A stereotype that causes a person to act in a manner that is consistent with that stereotype is called
   a. an illusory correlation.
   b. an illusion of out-group homogeneity.
   c. attributional bias.
   d. a self-fulfilling prophecy.

15.8. One explanation for the failure of people to come to the aid of a person in need, particular when others are present is
 a. deindividuation.
 b. social loafing.
 c. diffusion of responsibility.
 d. groupthink.

15.9. The tendency to become a social loafer is greater among _____ than it is among _____, and greater for people living in _____ cultures than people living in _____ cultures.
 a. men; women; Eastern; Western
 b. men; women; Western; Eastern
 c. women; men; Eastern; Western
 d. women; men; Western; Eastern

15.10. When the subject and learner were placed in different rooms, what percentage of subjects in Milgram's obedience study gave the learner what they believed to be a 450 volt electric shock?
 a. 30
 b. 40
 c. 50
 d. 60

15.11. The likely decision-making outcomes of groupthink include all of the following EXCEPT
 a. the illusion of invulnerability.
 b. the failure to consider the risks involved.
 c. incomplete or no research on the issue at hand.
 d. a failure to examine alternative courses of action.

15.12. The men in the Dutton and Aron study who were interviewed by the woman on the suspension bridge
 a. reported high levels of anxiety because of their fear of heights.
 b. reported low levels of anxiety, presumably because of the drug the researcher had given them.
 c. were reported by the woman to be of only average looks.
 d. were attracted to her.

Practice Tests
CHAPTER 15: Practice Test 2

15.13. Which of the following statements is TRUE?
 a. At the core of the self-concept is the self.
 b. Thinking of ourselves as we are at present accurately reflects our potential selves.
 c. People in Western cultures emphasize the relatedness of individuals to each other.
 d. Each of us has many potential selves that we might become, depending on our experience.

15.14. _____ is the aspect of attribution that focuses on the extent to which a person's behavior is similar across both time and settings.
 a. Consistency
 b. Consensus
 c. Distinctiveness
 d. Discounting

15.15. Suppose that you have a lot of friends who do not drink alcoholic beverages. Suppose further that you are asked in a class to answer the following question: "How many people do you think drink alcoholic beverages?" You reply, "Not many," based on the number of your friends who imbibe. In this case you have made an error based on your use of the _____ heuristic.
 a. representativeness
 b. availability
 c. general
 d. similarity

15.16. Attitudes that are formed by observing the emotional responses of others are learned through the process of _____ classical conditioning.
 a. vicarious
 b. direct
 c. implicit
 d. explicit

15.17. According to Festinger, inconsistencies between behavior and cognitions give rise to _____, which motivate(s) a person to _____ it.
 a. confusion and apathy; reduce
 b. counterattitudinal behavior; increase
 c. dissonance; reduce
 d. arousal; increase

15.18. The results of Sherif's classic study involving young campers suggests that prejudice is increased by _____ and decreased by _____.
 a. competition; cooperation
 b. collaboration; cooperation
 c. cooperation; competition
 d. cooperation; collaboration

15.19. A person who acts like he or she is a subject in an experiment but who is really an assistant of the experimenter is called a(n)
a. stooge.
b. experimental decoy.
c. accomplice.
d. confederate.

15.20. Zajonc's explanation of social facilitation centers on the idea of
a. competence.
b. compliance.
c. social norms.
d. arousal.

15.21. Suppose that you are asked by a charity to donate a few dollars to its cause (and you do). Suppose also, that afterwards, the charity approaches you again and asks you to donate several thousand dollars more. The technique that this charity is using to get you to comply with their request is called the _____ technique.
a. door-in-the-face
b. low-balling
c. foot-in-the-door
d. norm of reciprocity

15.22. The tendency for the initial feelings or thoughts of a group to become exaggerated during a discussion that precedes a decision is called
a. groupthink.
b. group mindset.
c. group tilt.
d. group polarization.

15.23. A person who likes cooking, gardening, and ice hockey is most likely to be attracted to a person who likes
a. eating pizza and drinking while watching bowling on television.
b. to do similar activities.
c. to do things other than cooking, gardening, and watching ice hockey.
d. opposite sorts of activities.

15.24. According to Sternberg, romantic love includes
a. intimacy and passion.
b. intimacy and commitment.
c. passion and commitment.
d. intimacy, passion, and commitment.

Practice Test Answers
CHAPTER 15: Practice Test 1

15.1. b, p. 486   By definition, the self is the term used to represent a person's distinct individuality.

15.2. b, p. 487   The causes of behavior can only originate from two sources or their interaction: factors internal to the person and factors external to the person.

15.3. b, p. 489   By definition the actor-observer effect is the tendency of people to explain their own behavior in terms of situational factors and other people's behavior in terms of dispositional factors.

15.4. b, p. 492   A person who has personal experience with a person, place or thing is said to acquire an attitude with respect to those factors through direct classical conditioning.

15.5. b, p. 494   By definition, a self-attribution is an attribution we make about our own behavior based on a self-observation of that behavior. In this example, we may conclude that our attitude toward people "into" body piercing is negative based on our self-observation that we tend to recoil when we see these people.

15.6. c, p. 497   By definition, self-perception theory states that we learn to understand our attitudes and emotions through self-observation of our behavior and the conditions under which it occurs.

15.7. d, p. 501   By definition, a self-fulfilling prophecy is a stereotype that causes a person to act in a manner that is consistent with that stereotype.

15.8. c, p. 504   People who fail to help a person in need often do so because they think that somebody in the crowd will come to that person's aid, a phenomenon that is called diffusion of responsibility.

15.9. b, p. 506   The are large gender and cultural differences in social loafing. Research has shown the tendency is greater for men than for women and for Westerners than for Easterners.

15.10. d, p. 509   Milgram's research results showed that 60 percent of his subjects were willing to administer what they thought was a 450 volt electric shock to the "learner."

15.11. a, p. 512   As Figure 5.10 shows, likely decision-making outcomes of groupthink do not include the illusion of invulnerability. The illusion of invulnerability is a symptom of groupthink

15.12. d, p. 516   Dutton and Aron's research results showed that the men who met the woman on the suspension bridge were, in fact, attracted to her. The evidence for this is that they were likely to call her later.

Practice Test Answers
CHAPTER 15: Practice Test 2

15.13. d, p. 486   People tend to think of themselves as having "working" self-concepts; that is, they see themselves has having different potential selves.

15.14. a, p. 488   By definition, consistency is that aspect of attribution that stresses the similarity of behavior across both time and circumstance.

15.15. b, p. 491   The availability heuristic refers to a general strategy we use for making decisions regarding the likelihood or the importance of an event based on the ease with which information regarding the issue is brought to mind. In this case, we say that most people don't drink because we have observed that none of our friends do (which, of course, is likely to be a biased sample).

15.16. a, p. 493   By definition, vicarious classical conditioning is the process of learning an attitude by observing how others react to a person, place or thing (no direct experience with these factors is involved).

15.17. c, p. 496   By definition, cognitive dissonance is produced by an inconsistency between thought and behavior, and serves as a source of motivation for people to reduce it.

15.18. a, p. 499   The results of Sherif's study showed that prejudice in a group of summer campers could be increased by assigning them to teams who competed against one another and reduced by inducing the teams to cooperate to solve an important problem.

15.19. d, p. 503   By definition, a confederate is an accomplice of the experimenter.

15.20. d, p. 505   Zajonc argued that the presence of others creates a heightened state of arousal while we are performing a task. If the task is well-practiced, then the arousal enhances our performance; if not, arousal impedes it.

15.21. c, p. 507   By definition, the foot-in-the-door technique is involves preceding a large, unreasonable request with a smaller, more reasonable one. In this case, the charity's request for the larger, unreasonable donation was preceded by the request for a smaller, more reasonable donation.

15.22. d, p. 511   By definition, group polarization is the tendency for the initial thoughts or feelings of a group to become exaggerated during a discussion that precedes a decision related to those thoughts or feelings.

15.23. b, p. 514   People are attracted to those who are similar to them in terms of interests, attitudes, and physical attractiveness.

15.24. a, p. 517   By Sternberg's definition, romantic love is the combination of intimacy and passion.

Practice Tests
CHAPTER 16: Practice Test 1

16.1. Many unhealthy behaviors that may be part of our lifestyles are acquired and maintained because they
   a. are not subject to the law of effect.
   b. do not have immediately negative consequences.
   c. are perceived as actually being healthy.
   d. are part of our genetic endowments.

16.2. Paffenbarger's research showed that on average, subjects who exercised _____ lived about _____ than subjects who exercised _____.
   a. rigorously; 3 years longer; moderately
   b. only slightly; 1 year longer; rigorously
   c. moderately; two years longer; only slightly
   d. moderately; 4 years longer; only slightly

16.3. People who switch from smoking high-nicotine cigarettes to smoking low-nicotine cigarettes
   a. dramatically reduce their chances of suffering from cancer and other smoking-related illnesses.
   b. actually smoke more cigarettes to compensate for the loss of nicotine.
   c. report that they enjoy the psychological benefits of smoking more now than when they were smoking the high-nicotine cigarettes.
   d. no longer enjoy smoking as much as they did before they switched.

16.4. Liam is taking Percodan to help relieve the pain he is experiencing from the extraction of a wisdom tooth earlier in the day. The drug is effective in reducing the pain, and Liam decides he will go out for the evening with a few friends. Liam has several beers. Unknowingly, Liam is running the risk of death due to
   a. a heart attack.
   b. failure of the circulatory system.
   c. failure of the respiratory system.
   d. massive internal bleeding.

16.5. Which of the following statements is FALSE?
   a. AIDS may be transmitted through casual contact.
   b. AIDS appeared suddenly and without warning.
   c. Many people see themselves as being at risk for contracting AIDS.
   d. Researchers do not yet understanding AIDS well enough to develop a cure for it.

16.6. Lyle wants to buy a new CD system. Every week he cashes his paycheck and deposits part of it into a coffee can at home. Sometimes, though, he is unable to put anything away for the CD system because he spends the money on movies, pizza, clothes, and other things that he likes but doesn't really need. In this example, the long-term reward is
   a. his paycheck.
   b. the money he spends on movies, pizza, and other things.
   c. the purchase of the CD player.
   d. all of the above

16.7. The stage of the General Adaptation Syndrome in which the organism may experience shock is called the _____ stage.
a. alarm reaction
b. adaptation reaction
c. stage of resistance
d. stage of exhaustion

16.8. An example of a glucocorticoid is
a. cortisol.
b. epinephrine.
c. norepinephrine.
d. reserpine.

16.9. Hardiness seems to develop as a result of
a. parental warmth.
b. a stimulating home environment.
c. family support in solving problems of moderate difficulty.
d. all of the above

16.10. The reaction of the immune system that involves antibodies is called a(n) _____ reaction.
a. cell-mediated
b. chemically mediated
c. immuno-
d. lymphocyte

16.11. Rhonda has a family history of cancer and recently discovered a lump in her breast. What would be the best advice to give Rhonda?
a. think positively.
b. get medical treatment soon.
c. visualize the white blood cells killing the cancer cells.
d. ignore the lump and pretend it does not really exist.

16.12. Amy visits the student mental health center to talk to a counselor about her test anxiety. The counselor teaches Amy to relax various muscles in her body when she begins to feel tense. The counselor has taught Amy how to use _____ to cope with stress.
a. cognitive reappraisal
b. aerobic exercise
c. progressive relaxation
d. an emotion-focused coping strategy

Practice Tests
CHAPTER 16: Practice Test 2

16.13. Which of the following countries has a relatively low rate of death due to breast cancer (and a correlated low intake of fat)?
   a. Mexico
   b. Norway
   c. the United States
   d. Denmark

16.14. Cigarette smoking appears to be maintained, at least in part, by
   a. positive reinforcement.
   b. imitation.
   c. both positive and negative reinforcement.
   d. all of the above

16.15. About _____ of all alcohol consumed in the U.S. is consumed by about _____ of all drinkers.
   a. one-quarter; one-eighth
   b. one-third; one-half
   c. one-half; one-tenth
   d. three-quarters; one-fourth

16.16. Which of the following is a goal of STD prevention programs?
   a. familiarize people with safe sex practices
   b. teach people the connection between their behavior and getting an STD or AIDS
   c. provide support and encouragement for safe sex practices
   d. all of the above

16.17. In communities where Geller's seat belt program has been used and then discontinued, rates of seat belt usage
   a. stays about the same.
   b. declines slowly back to rates prior to the implementation of the program.
   c. declines rapidly back to rates prior to the implementation of the program.
   d. declines, but not back to rates prior to the implementation of the program.

16.18. According to the model of self-control described in the text, the best way to exert self-control is to move the moment of decision to
   a. a time before the value of the small, short-term reward exceeds the value of the larger, long-term reward.
   b. a time after the value of the small, short-term reward exceeds the value of the larger, long-term reward.
   c. a time after the value of the small, short-term reward is equal to the value of the larger, long-term reward.
   d. a time before the value of the larger, long-term reward exceeds the value of the small, short-term reward.

16.19. About two months ago, Ariel and Arlo's mobile home was destroyed by a fire. About a week ago, both of them started getting sick: they both have colds, feel run-down, and are complaining of stomach problems. Which stage of the General Adaptation Syndrome are they experiencing?
    a. alarm reaction
    b. adaptation reaction
    c. stage of resistance
    d. stage of exhaustion

16.20. The effect that certain stressors, such as those that cause anxiety and fear, have on a person depends on his or her
    a. behavioral responsiveness.
    b. level of physical fitness.
    c. perception and emotional reactivity.
    d. lifestyle and expectations for success.

16.21. Research on personality variables and the risk of coronary heart disease have determined that
    a. health and life-style variables cannot be separated from personality variables.
    b. coronary heart disease is too complex to be caused only by personality variables.
    c. personality variables do not affect the risk of coronary heart disease.
    d. personality variables are important, but the exact nature of the relationship is unclear.

16.22. The immunoglobulin known as IgA is
    a. found in lower than normal levels when a person is happy.
    b. not directly involved in the operation of the human immune system.
    c. present in the secretions of the mucous membranes.
    d. all of the above

16.23. Mrs. Leyland always gets extremely nervous when her 11-year-old son, Trent, is up to bat. As soon as he steps into the batter's box, she gets up and walks to a place behind the stands where she cannot see him. This relaxes her a bit; she returns to the stands when she thinks that her son has finished batting. The coping style used by Mrs. Leyland is called _____-focused coping.
    a. problem
    b. emotion
    c. solution
    d. situation

16.24. The stress management program that helps people develop coping skills that help increase their resistance to the negative effects of stress is called stress _____ training.
    a. resistance
    b. prevention
    c. inoculation
    d. education

Practice Test Answers
CHAPTER 16: Practice Test 1

16.1.   b, p. 526   Many unhealthy behaviors, for example, cigarette smoking, have pleasurable effects in the short-run, but negative effects in the long run.

16.2.   c, p. 528   Paffenbarger's research did, in fact, show that people who exercise the equivalent of running or walking five miles a week live, on average, about two years longer than more sedentary people.

16.3.   b, p. 530   The bodies of cigarette smokers who switch from smoking high-nicotine cigarettes to smoking low-nicotine cigarettes experience withdrawal from the higher levels of nicotine. In order to satisfy the body's craving for more nicotine, the individual smokes more low-nicotine cigarettes.

16.4.   c, p. 533   Mixing a narcotic, such as Percodan, with alcohol can lead to death by respiratory failure.

16.5.   a, p. 535   Numerous research studies have shown that AIDS cannot be transmitted through casual contact. It can only be transmitted through sexual relations or through AIDS-contaminated blood that makes contact with an uninfected individual's blood.

16.6.   c, p. 537   By definition, the long-term reward is that reward that is obtainable only after a certain amount of time has passed and exceeds the value of smaller rewards that are available immediately. In this case, the obtaining of a new CD system fits this definition.

16.7.   a, p. 540   By definition the alarm stage of the General Adaptation Syndrome involves the possibility of the organism experiencing shock.

16.8.   a, p. 541   Cortisol is classified as a glucocorticoid.

16.9.   d, p. 543   Kobasa's research has shown that the people most likely to develop hardy personalities are those who experienced a stimulating, warm, and supportive home environment while they were growing up.

16.10.   b, p. 545   By definition, a chemically mediated reaction is any immune system reaction that involves antibodies.

16.11.   b, p. 550   Any woman who finds a lump in her breast should consult a physician immediately.

16.12.   c, p. 553   Persons, such as Amy, who have learned to cope with a stressor by using the presence of that stressor as a signal to start relaxing have most likely been trained in the use of progressive relaxation techniques.

Practice Test Answers
CHAPTER 16: Practice Test 2

16.13.   a, p. 527   As Figure 16.1 on page 527 clearly shows, of the countries listed, only Mexico has a relatively low rate of death due to breast cancer.

16.14.   c, p. 530   Cigarette smoking produces positive reinforcement in the form of the pleasures derived from smoking and involves negative reinforcement in that people continue to smoke, in part, because they wish to avoid the unpleasant bodily reactions that accompany reduced nicotine consumption.

16.15.   c, p. 531   Statistical analysis of patterns of drinking show that a tenth of the people who drink alcoholic beverages consume about half of the total alcohol ingested in the U.S.

16.16.   d, p. 534   The purpose of all STD prevention programs is to introduce people to safe sex practices, provide support and encouragement for these practices, and to teach people that contracting an STD or AIDS can be a result of unsafe sexual behavior.

16.17.   d, p. 536   Geller's own research on seat belt usage shows that when his seat belt program is discontinued, seat belt usage decreases, but not back to levels prior to the implementation of the program.

16.18.   a, p. 538   People who commit to obtaining the long-term reward in such a way as to prevent temptation by the short-term reward are likely to exhibit high levels of self-control. The best way to make this commitment is to move the moment of decision to a time prior to the value of the short-term reward becoming temporarily larger than the value of the long-term reward.

16.19.   d, p. 540   By definition, the stage of exhaustion of the General Adaptation Syndrome involves illness of the variety experienced by Ariel and Arlo.

16.20.   c, p. 542   Research investigating the effects of stressors on behavior has revealed that one's perception and level of emotional reactivity to the stressor is related to the degree of fear and anxiety caused by stressor. People with a high level of emotional reactivity, and who perceive a stressor as threatening, experience high levels of fear and anxiety.

16.21.   d, p. 544   After much research on the relationship between personality factors and coronary heart disease, investigators are still not sure of the precise nature of the relationship. There is little doubt that personality factors are important in the development of coronary heart disease, but the exact role they play is presently unknown.

16.22.   c, p. 547   IgA is, in fact, present in secretions of the mucous membranes. When IgA levels are suppressed, people become more susceptible to respiratory infections.

16.23.   b, p. 552   By definition, emotion-focused coping involves behaviors aimed at changing one's own emotional reaction to a stressor, which is the strategy Mrs. Leyland adopts when she removes herself from the stands to a place where she cannot see her son batting.

16.24.   c, p. 554   By definition, stress inoculation training is a stress management program that aids people in developing specific coping skills to increase resistance to the negative effects of stress.

Practice Tests
CHAPTER 17: Practice Test 1

17.1. Erin is a clinical psychologist who specializes in researching mental disorders. She views most disorders as being due to both genetic predisposition and environmental influences. Erin subscribes to the _____ model of mental disorders.
   a. ultimate-proximate
   b. genotype-phenotype
   c. diathesis-stress
   d. medical

17.2. A problem with the DSM-IV system of classifying mental disorders is its
   a. emphasis on clinical and personality disorders.
   b. reliability.
   c. use of only five axes.
   d. all of the above

17.3. The three most prevalent mental disorders in the U.S. are _____ disorders.
   a. personality, schizophrenic, and mood
   b. antisocial personality, mood, and anxiety
   c. schizophrenia, mood, and dissociative
   d. mood, anxiety, and substance abuse

17.4. Women are _____ times more likely than men to develop panic disorder. The disorder usually begins in _____, and rarely after the age of _____.
   a. two; early adulthood; 35
   b. three; middle adulthood; 50
   c. two; adolescence; 20
   d. three; middle adulthood; 35

17.5. Which of the following is NOT one of the four categories into which most compulsions fall?
   a. avoidance
   b. checking
   c. counting
   d. obsessing

17.6. The culture-bound syndrome known as nangiarpok seems similar to what is described in the DSM-IV as a
   a. somatization disorder.
   b. phobia.
   c. personality disorder.
   d. dissociative disorder.

17.7. People who commit serious crimes because they "just felt like it" may suffer from a psychological disorder called
   a. paranoid schizophrenia.
   b. psychogenic fugue.
   c. antisocial personality disorder.
   d. conversion disorder.

17.8. Betty doesn't drink very often, but when she does, she tends to drink a lot. It seems that once she starts drinking, she cannot stop until she gets extremely drunk. Psychologists would classify Betty as a _____ drinker.
   a. social
   b. abusive
   c. binge
   d. steady

17.9. Archie is a student of mine who believes that I am manipulating his thoughts and actions. Archie appears to be experiencing delusions of
   a. grandeur.
   b. control.
   c. persecution.
   d. power.

17.10. Who is most likely to be diagnosed as having schizophrenia?
   a. the spouse of a person with schizophrenia
   b. the nephew or niece of a person with schizophrenia
   c. the sibling of a person with schizophrenia
   d. an individual unrelated to a person with schizophrenia

17.11. Expressed emotion includes expressions of _____ by family members toward a relative having schizophrenia.
   a. criticism and hostility
   b. love and compassion
   c. concern and empathy
   d. constructive criticism and realistic emotional support

17.12. Which of the following is NOT described in the text as being a possible etiological factor in mood disorders?
   a. faulty cognition
   b. heredity
   c. patterns of family interaction
   d. sleep/wake cycles

Practice Tests
CHAPTER 17: Practice Test 2

17.13.   Factitious mental disorders are disorders that
    a. involve a loss of personal identity.
    b. involve pain.
    c. involve fetishes.
    d. are fake.

17.14.   The development of successful treatment programs for different disorders is often preceded by
    a. a knowledge of their specific causes.
    b. extensive etiological research.
    c. discovery of "cures" for those disorders.
    d. placing those disorders into specific diagnostic categories.

17.15.   Actuarial judgments are more accurate than clinical judgments because
    a. clinical judgments are influenced by information that is salient to the therapist.
    b. therapists do not always produce the same judgment of different circumstances.
    c. therapists often draw conclusions based on preestablished hypotheses.
    d. all of the above

17.16.   Men and women are equally like to develop _____ but women are more likely than men to develop _____.
    a. a simple phobia; a specific phobia
    b. claustrophobia; acrophobia
    c. a specific phobia; a simple phobia
    d. a social phobia; agoraphobia

17.17.   People with conversion disorder
    a. are generally in their middle to late 40s.
    b. often suffer from symptoms of diseases with which they are familiar.
    c. are most often female.
    d. all of the above

17.18.   A person who is self-promoting, shows little empathy for others, and seeks attention for himself or herself is exhibiting symptoms of _____ personality disorder.
    a. narcissistic
    b. avoidant
    c. passive-aggressive
    d. histrionic

17.19.   Children with conduct problems who later develop the symptoms of antisocial personality disorder tend to
    a. perceive their environment as being hostile and threatening.
    b. be latch-key children, who are unsupervised after school lets out for the day.
    c. engage in sexual fantasies more than "normal" children.
    d. all of the above

17.20. Research using rats as subjects has shown that alcohol produces a larger release of _____ in the brains of alcohol-preferring rats than in the brains of non-alcohol-preferring rats.
a. serotonin
b. monoamine oxidase inhibitors
c. dopamine
d. atropine

17.21. According to Bleuler, _____ schizophrenia is a form of schizophrenia that has a rapid onset and a brief duration.
a. undifferentiated
b. reactive
c. process
d. disorganized

17.22. Based on research using imaging devices, the brains of persons having schizophrenia appear to differ from the brains of those persons who do not have schizophrenia in that they (the brains of persons having schizophrenia)
a. contain less brain tissue.
b. contain more brain tissue.
c. show deformities of the limbic system.
d. show erratic firing of unmyelinated neurons.

17.23. In between bouts of depression and mania, people having bipolar disorder generally
a. feel slightly depressed.
b. feel slightly euphoric.
c. develop amnesia regarding their mood swings.
d. exhibit normal behavior.

17.24. A drug called _____ is effective in combating the symptoms of _____.
a. chlorpromazine; depression
b. reserpine; depression
c. imipramine; bipolar disorder
d. lithium carbonate; bipolar disorder

Practice Test Answers
CHAPTER 17: Practice Test 1

17.1.   c, p. 564   By definition, the diathesis stress model of mental disorders attributes the onset of a mental disorder to the interaction of genetic and environmental factors, a view held in this example by Erin.

17.2.   b, p. 566   Because interpretation of the symptoms and the severity of a mental disorder is subjective, use of the DSM-IV is less than perfectly reliable in the diagnosis of mental disorders.

17.3.   d, p. 567   The statistical data presented in Table 17.2 on page 567 show that the three most prevalent mental disorders in the U.S. are, in order, substance abuse disorders, anxiety disorders, and mood disorders.

17.4.   a, p. 571   Demographic data gathered on people who suffer from mental disorders reveal that women are twice as likely as men to suffer from panic disorder and that this disorder usually develops in early adulthood but before a person is 35-years-old.

17.5.   d, p. 573   Most compulsions fall into four categories: counting, checking, cleaning, and avoidance. Obsessions are not considered to be a compulsion.

17.6.   b, p. 579   By definition, a phobia is an excessive and irrational fear of some person, place, or thing. Nangiarpok is an excessive and irrational fear of being trapped and drowning in a capsized kayak.

17.7.   c, p. 581   One symptom of antisocial personality disorder is that the person has no reason for committing an antisocial act other than because he or she "just felt like it."

17.8.   c, p. 584   By definition, binge drinkers are people who can go without drinking for a long time, but when they do to drink, they are unable to control themselves. Betty, in this example, fits this profile.

17.9.   b, p. 586   By definition, a delusion of control involves the mistaken belief that a person is being controlled or manipulated by others. In this example, Archie fits this description.

17.10.   c, p. 588   The likelihood of being diagnosed as having schizophrenia increases as the degree of genetic relatedness to a person already diagnosed as having this disorder increases. Of the alternative answers listed in this case, the sibling of a person having schizophrenia faces the greatest risk of developing the disorder.

17.11.   a, p. 592   By definition, expressed emotion involves expressions of criticism and hostility. It also includes emotional overinvolvement on the part of family members toward a relative having schizophrenia.

17.12.   c, p. 594   Research has established that the most likely factors involved in the etiology of mood disorders are faulty cognitions, genetic factors, and sleep/wake cycles. Patterns of family interactions have not been established as a risk factor in mood disorders.

Practice Test Answers
CHAPTER 17: Practice Test 2

17.13.   d, p. 565   By definition, factitious disorders are fake mental disorders such as Munchausen syndrome.

17.14.   d, p. 566   As in all areas of scientific endeavor, explanation of a problem or issue is made easier by first providing an accurate description of the problem or issue. The same is true for developing a successful treatment program for a mental disorder.

17.15.   d, p. 568   Actuarial judgments are made on the basis of objective statistical information about a state of affairs. Clinical judgments are necessarily more subjective and less accurate because of the inherit biases of the person making them.

17.16.   d, p. 572   Demographic data reveal that although men and women are equally likely to develop a social phobia, women are more likely than men to develop agoraphobia.

17.17.   b, p. 576   Research on conversion disorders has revealed that people who suffer from conversion disorder develop symptoms of diseases and illnesses with which they are already familiar.

17.18.   a, p. 580   By definition, the symptoms of a narcissistic personality disorder include self-promotion, lack of empathy for others, and attention seeking.

17.19.   a, p. 582   Research on children who have conduct problems and who later develop antisocial personality disorder often perceive their environments as being hostile and threatening relative to children who do not have conduct problems.

17.20.   c, p. 585   Fadda et al.'s research revealed that alcohol caused the brains of alcohol-preferring rats to produce increases in the secretion of dopamine.

17.21.   b, p. 588   By Bleuler's definition, reactive schizophrenia has a sudden onset and lasts only a short time.

17.22.   a, p. 590   Brain scans of the brains of both non-psychotic people and those with schizophrenia have shown that the brains of schizophrenics contain less brain tissue than the brains of non-psychotic people.

17.23.   d, p. 593   Studies of people with bipolar disorder have found that these people do not constantly suffer from depression or mania. Instead, in between periods of depression and periods of mania, these people experience periods of normalcy.

17.24.   d, p. 595   Lithium carbonate is the drug of choice for the treatment of bipolar disorder.

Practice Tests
CHAPTER 18: Practice Test 1

18.1. Therapy is intended for those people who
    a. have severe psychological problems.
    b. desire to improve the quality of their life.
    c. have trouble relating to others.
    d. all of the above

18.2. Freud believed that transference is beneficial to the therapeutic process because it
    a. allows the therapist to become more objectively involved in the personal aspects of the client's life.
    b. provides a medium through which the client relives important early experiences.
    c. is cathartic.
    d. elevates the client's mood.

18.3. LaTosha is young, affluent, intelligent, and suffering from mild depression. Lacey is older, less well off financially, less intelligent, and is suffering from a severe form of schizophrenia. Who is the better candidate for psychodynamic therapy?
    a. LaTosha
    b. Lacey
    c. both
    d. neither

18.4. Disulfiram is a drug that is sometimes used to treat alcoholism. When ingested, this drug will cause the person to become sick if he or she drinks an alcoholic beverage. This approach to treating alcoholism is an example of
    a. implosion therapy.
    b. rational-emotive therapy.
    c. systematic desensitization.
    d. aversion therapy.

18.5. Assertiveness therapy is especially effective for people who
    a. have difficulty standing up for themselves.
    b. have difficulty getting their point across to other people.
    c. feel frustrated because nobody pays attention to them.
    d. all of the above

18.6. The first form of cognitive restructuring, which is called _____ was developed by _____.
    a. cognitive -behavior therapy; Rogers
    b. cognitive therapy for depression; Beck
    c. rational-emotive therapy; Ellis
    d. covert sensitization; Wolpe

18.7. In Beck's view, a person's negative beliefs are a result of his or her
    a. imitation of others' actions.
    b. internal locus of control.
    c. faulty logic.
    d. low degree of self-efficacy.

18.8. The basic assumption of family therapy is that problems arise
   a. because of problems with parental discipline methods.
   b. out of patterns of family interactions.
   c. from irrational family belief systems.
   d. because of a child's irresponsible behavior.

18.9. The prompt identification of a problem, along with immediate attempts to intervene before the problem worsens, is the objective of programs emphasizing
   a. primary prevention.
   b. secondary prevention.
   c. tertiary prevention.
   d. deinstitutionalization.

18.10. A critical difference between an ineffective therapist and an effective therapist is the ability to
   a. understand the client's problems.
   b. establish a warm, understanding, and empathetic relationship with the client.
   c. guarantee the client that his or her problems will remain confidential.
   d. all of the above

18.11. One effect of tricyclic drugs and monamine oxidase inhibitors is to
   a. reduce the symptoms of anxiety.
   b. reduce mania.
   c. elevate mood.
   d. reduce attentional deficits.

18.12. The therapeutic benefit of ECT rests in the _____ it produces.
   a. seizures
   b. convulsions
   c. decreases in GABA levels
   d. changes in the electrical activity of the thalamus

Practice Tests
CHAPTER 18: Practice Test 2

18.13. Last night Connie dreamed that the hot water tank located in the attic burst and flooded the house. The bursting of the hot water heater and the flooding of the house constitute the _____ content of the dream.
   a. symbolic
   b. latent
   c. submerged
   d. manifest

18.14. Consider the brief transcript below, which was taken from a therapy session involving a 19-year-old college student suffering from anxiety.

   C: Sometimes I can't stand school. There's so much pressure and so many tests and papers; the work never seems to end. There's always another deadline to meet. It's really getting to me.
   T: Sounds to me like you're saying that you need a break, perhaps a long weekend at the beach?

   What therapeutic technique was the therapist using?
   a. congruence.
   b. cognitive restructuring.
   c. systematic desensitization.
   d. reflection.

18.15. The therapy procedure that begins with the client making a list of stimuli that are ranked in order of their ability to produce anxiety is called
   a. rational-emotive therapy.
   b. aversion therapy.
   c. modeling.
   d. systematic desensitization.

18.16. Token economies are sometimes difficult to implement because
   a. they are extremely complicated.
   b. staff persons may not understand how the system works or agree that it is a good system.
   c. they are expensive to operate.
   d. all of the above

18.17. Lynette is a cigarette smoker who desires to quit smoking. She has tried several times to quit on her own, but so far has failed. She decides to consult a therapist. Her therapist suggests that she imagine herself dying of lung cancer and the anguish her dying causes her loved ones. Lynette's therapist is using a method of therapy called
   a. aversion therapy.
   d. covert sensitization.
   b. punishment therapy.
   c. rational-emotive therapy.

18.18. Rational-emotive therapy has been shown to be effective in the treatment of
   a. test anxiety.
   b. depression.
   c. schizophrenia.
   d. severe anxiety.

18.19. In order to infer the nature of the interrelationships within a family, the family therapist will
a. collect data about the interactions among family members.
b. interview each family member.
c. give family members personality tests.
d. all of the above

18.20. A community treatment program that functions primarily to help make the transition from living in a mental institution to living in a regular community is the
a. community mission.
b. group home.
c. halfway house.
d. community mental health center.

18.21. A western therapist who is confronted with a client who is suffering from a mental disorder and whose belief system appears to be culture-bound may find that _____ is the most effective approach to providing treatment.
a. combining traditional psychotherapy with indigenous healing therapy
b. drug therapy
c. tradition forms of therapy
d. combining rational-emotive therapy with Beck's cognitive therapy for depression

18.22. The biochemical basis of schizophrenia, at least as far as the positive symptoms of the disorder are concerned, involve
a. overactivity of dopamine receptors.
b. underactivity of norepinephrine receptors.
c. depletion of serotonin.
d. underproduction of acetylcholine.

18.23. MAOIs exerts their therapeutic effect by
a. retarding the reuptake of norepinephrine and serotonin.
b. stimulating the production of norepinephrine and serotonin.
c. preventing enzymes in the synaptic gap from destroying dopamine, norepinephrine and serotonin.
d. blocking postsynaptic receptors sensitive to norepinephrine and serotonin.

18.24. Unalterable brain surgery that is intended to reduce the symptoms of mental disorders is called
a. psychosurgery.
b. neurosurgery.
c. cerebralsurgery.
d. all of the above

Practice Test Answers
CHAPTER 18: Practice Test 1

18.1. d, p. 605   Psychological therapy may be of benefit to people who have severe psychological problems, people who desire to improve their quality of life, and people who have difficulty relating to others.

18.2. b, p. 607   Freud argued that transference, or the client's projection of emotion and attitudes onto the therapist, helps the client relive traumatic experiences that occurred earlier in life.

18.3. a, p. 609   Psychodynamic therapy best benefits those people who are intelligent, articulate, financially capable, and who do not suffer from severe psychological problems. Given these criteria, LaTosha is the better candidate for this form of therapy.

18.4. d, p. 612   Aversion therapy involves training the client to respond negatively to a neutral stimulus that has been paired with an aversive stimulus. In this case, the consumption of an alcoholic beverage becomes associated with the illness produced when alcohol is combined with disulfiram.

18.5. d, p. 614   The people most likely to benefit from undergoing assertiveness therapy are those who shy away from standing up for themselves, have difficulty getting their points across to others, or are ignored by others.

18.6. c, p. 616   Albert Ellis developed rational-emotive therapy in the 1950s, long before the phrase *cognitive restructuring* was even coined. Rational-emotive therapy is considered by many psychologists to be the forerunner of therapies based on cognitive restructuring.

18.7. c, p. 618   Beck views the cognitive triad as being the result of faulty logic; that is, depressed people tend to draw wrongheaded conclusions based on logical mistakes.

18.8. b, p. 621   A fundamental reason why family therapists are so interested in talking to family members of the person who presents for therapy is they hold the assumption that this person's problems derive from interactions with other family members. In other words, the problem that is presented for treatment extends beyond a single individual into the family context.

18.9. b, p. 623   By definition, secondary prevention involves the immediate identification of problems and the prompt implementation of intervention strategies to address those problems.

18.10. b, p. 627   Researchers who have examined the key factors involved in the effectiveness of therapy in treating a client's problems have found that all effective interventions involve the establishment of a warm, understanding, and empathetic relationship between the therapist and client.

18.11. c, p. 631   Tricyclic drugs retard reuptake of serotonin and norepinephrine and monoamine oxidase inhibitors prevent enzymes in the synaptic gap from destroying dopamine, serotonin, and norepinephrine. The effect of increases in these transmitter substances at postsynaptic receptor sites is an elevation in mood.

18.12. a, p. 632   Research evidence reveals that it is the seizure activity produced by ECT therapy, and nothing else, that produces the therapeutic effect in this form of treatment for depression.

Practice Test Answers
CHAPTER 18: Practice Test 2

18.13. d, p. 606 By definition, the manifest content of a dream includes the actual images contained in the dream. In this example, these images include the bursting of the hot water heater and the flooding of the house.

18.14. d, p. 608 By definition, reflection is the therapist's restatement of the client's observations. In this example, the therapist is reflecting the client's statements about problems associated with school.

18.15. d, p. 611 By definition, systematic desensitization involves the client making a hierarchical ranking of the stimuli that make him or her fearful or anxious.

18.16. d, p. 613 The effectiveness of a token economy can be easily sabotaged by its complexity and cost, as well as by resistance among hospital staff and others who either don't understand the system or who resist its implementation.

18.17. b, p. 615 By definition, covert sensitization involves a client imagining the aversive consequences of his or her inappropriate behavior. In this example, Lynn is told to image herself dying of lung cancer that develops because of her cigarette smoking.

18.18. a, p. 617 In general, research has established that rational-emotive therapy is effective in treating general anxiety, test anxiety, and unassertiveness.

18.19. a, p. 621 The most effective way that a family therapist can understand the interrelationships among family members is to collect data on how family members interact.

18.20. c, p. 622 By definition, a halfway house functions primarily to help people make the transition from living in a mental institution to living in a regular community setting.

18.21. a, p. 625 Therapists have discovered that the most effective means of treating people having a mental disorder and who hold traditional cultural beliefs is to use a combination of psychotherapy and indigenous healing therapy.

18.22. a, p. 630 Drugs that are used to treat schizophrenia reduce the positive symptoms of the disorder by reducing the amount of activity that occurs at dopamine receptors. Remember, the positive symptoms of this disorder are related to an overabundance of dopamine.

18.23. a, p. 631 MAOIs prevent enzymes in the synaptic gap from destroying dopamine, serotonin, and norepinephrine. Low levels of these transmitter substances are associated with depression.

18.24. a, p. 633 By definition, psychosurgery is unalterable brain surgery that is intended to lessen the symptoms of mental disorders.